Discipleship
by
Ron R. Ritchie

Discipleship (4th Edition)

Copyright © 2006, 2007, 2010, 2011 by Ron R. Ritchie

Free At Last JSU, Inc., PO Box 207 Menlo Park, CA 94026

ISBN-13: 978-1463715922 ISBN-10: 1463715927

www.ronritchie.com

The full sermon series on the Gospel of Luke, as preached from the pulpit at Peninsula Bible Church, is available on our web site.

Cover art by Rodd R. Ritchie (a photo taken during a tour of the Seven Churches of Revelation in October 2004).

" In the beginning..."

In 64 AD, the apostle Paul wrote to his spiritual son Timothy the following encouraging words:

You therefore, my son, be strong in the grace that is in Christ Jesus. The things which you have heard from me in the presence of many witnesses, entrust these to faithful men who will be able to teach others also. (2 Timothy 2:1-2)

In 1965, I celebrated my tenth year as a Christian and my third year of study at Dallas Theological Seminary. In that year, my *Prof*, Dr. Howard Hendricks, invited me to join him and some 13 other men to study together the *principles of discipleship.* I was delighted to be part of that study because I had never met a pastor during the previous ten years—within some nine churches that Anne Marie and I had attended and served—who had been committed to discipling men and women. It was in that same year that *Prof* invited all of us to a special weekend retreat to meet his best friend, Ray C. Stedman, who was also committed—along with the staff and elders of Peninsula Bible Church in Palo Alto, California—to discipling men and women for the work of ministry (Ephesians 4). When I graduated in 1966, I was invited to become the Director of Christian Education and Youth Pastor at Walnut Creek Presbyterian Church in Walnut Creek, California. By that time, I was fully committed to our Lord's command to His disciples in Matthew 28:18-20: *"All authority has been given to Me in heaven and on earth. Go therefore and make disciples of all the nations, baptizing them in the name of the Father and the Son and the Holy Spirit, teaching them to observe all that I commanded you; and lo, I am with you always, even to the end of the age."*
At the same time, I quickly discovered that I was but an hour away from Peninsula Bible Church, so I began taking weekly trips to meet with pastors Ray Stedman, Dave Roper and Bob Smith. They had taken our Lord's words about *making disciples* seriously among the members of PBC, and had begun an internship program. Those young men and women were willing to take time out of their busy lives to not only study the Word of God, but to be equipped to serve the Lord Jesus in a variety of ministries within the church and the community. (The Intern Program was either a one or two year commitment, which included being personally discipled by a staff member, attending weekly classes, holding down a part-time job and serving in ministry with their staff member.)

After three and a half years at Walnut Creek I was invited to join the staff of PBC in 1969 as a Youth Pastor. At that time, Dave Roper encouraged me to find some Interns to help with my new ministry. Ray, Dave and Bob had already set the model, so it was really a matter of trusting the Lord to help me find the Interns that He had in mind to help me shepherd our High School students. My first Intern was a young man named John Fischer who had just graduated from Wheaton College. He was soon followed by Dick and Jan Patterson, Patty Martin, Barry and Julie Smith, Donna Drury, Pam and Mark Hall and Pat McCallum, just to mention a few of the first of many faithful disciples. I am so grateful to the former faithful PBC staff and elders, who set the modern model for me and encouraged so many others like me to give our lives to discipling other men and women in our generation.

Eventually I took the PBC "on-campus" internship program off the campus and began inviting men and women from both the student and business communities to participate in *The Timothy Discipleship Experience* (which I'll explain in more detail in the following pages). Even now, some 40 years later, I am still involved in *making disciples* among God's flock.

The following pages are a compilation of materials I have been using to equip *disciples* for the work of ministry (Ephesians 4). My hope is that this booklet will encourage you to begin, where you are right now in fulfilling that Great Commission of Jesus Christ as recorded in Matthew 28:18-20.

Ron R. Ritchie
September 2007

Prayer

John R. W. Stott

Good morning, heavenly Father;
good morning, Lord Jesus;
good morning, Holy Spirit.

Heavenly Father, I worship you as the Creator and Sustainer of the universe.
Lord Jesus, I worship you, Savior and Lord of the world.
Holy Spirit, I worship you, Sanctifier of the people of God.
Glory to the Father, and to the Son, and to the Holy Spirit.
As it was in the beginning, is now, and will be forever. Amen.

Heavenly Father, I pray that I may live this day in your presence
  and please you more and more.
Lord Jesus, I pray that this day I may take up my cross and follow you.
Holy Spirit, I pray that this day you will fill me with yourself
  and cause your fruit to ripen in my life: love, joy, peace, patience, kindness,
  goodness, faithfulness, gentleness, and self-control.

Holy, blessed, and glorious Trinity, three persons in one God,
  have mercy upon me.
Amen.

Let's make sure the Main thing is the _Right_ Person!

The goal of all of our spiritual activity, whether it be personal, in groups, through prayer, Bible study, discipleship, attending worship services, retreats, mission trips, or serving the members of our immediate or spiritual family or our local community, has to be focused *not* on the **right** thing, but on the **right person**.

In 64 AD, the apostle Paul had been waiting for some two years in a Roman prison cell hoping to appear before Caesar Nero. As a Roman citizen, he had the right to appeal his case, which was based on some trumped up charges initiated by the Jewish religious leaders in Jerusalem some four years earlier (Acts 21:17-26:32). While he was awaiting his appearance before the court, he wrote an encouraging letter to his beloved spiritual family in the ancient city of Philippi (Acts 16:9-40) and he shared with them that he had discovered the goal of his life and ministry:

> *"...I count all things to be loss in view of the surpassing value **of knowing Christ Jesus my Lord**, for whom I have suffered the loss of all things, and count them but rubbish so that I may gain Christ, and may be found in Him, not having a righteousness of my own derived from the Law, but that which is through faith in Christ, the righteousness which comes from God on the basis of faith, **that I may know Him** and the power of His resurrection and the fellowship of His sufferings, being conformed to His death; in order that I may attain to the resurrection from the dead."* (Philippians 3: 8-11)

"By imitating Him, by sharing His experience, by living life as He lived it, allowing the Holy Spirit to shape you by the disciplines from the inside out, you will become more like Him." —*Chuck Swindoll*, an excerpt from "So, You Want To Be Like Christ?" © Copyright 2005, W Publishing Group, Nashville, TN. P. 16.

A Word of Gratitude

The time it has taken over the years to pray about, select, love, care for, teach and prepare men and women for a lifestyle of discipleshp has all been built on the model of our Lord Jesus Christ's life and teaching as recorded in the Gospels. His last words to his disciples, shortly after his resurrection and moments before his ascension into heaven, came in the form of a *command*: ***In your going make disciples...*** (Matthew 28:16-20). Once I made the decision to grow and mature in the understanding of our Lord's *command*, my faithful and loving wife **Anne Marie** has walked beside me through all of these years. In the following pages, you will have an opportunity to read about some of the others, such as **Ed Woodhall** and **Norm Nason** who were in discipleship groups, became co-disciplers with me over a period of several years, and are now leading their own groups, as well as other brothers and sisters who have come alongside to encourage us in our discipling ministry. I also want to thank the ***Free at Last*** Board Members, who are a daily encouragement in this ministry: ***Eff*** and ***Patty Martin, Frank VanderZwan, Norm Nason, Rob Faisant, Don Wood***, and ***Ron Robinson.*** I am also very grateful for the encouragement and support of our secretary, ***Irene Petersen***, who has worked so faithfully on this Discipleship manual.

Ron R. Ritchie

Ron R. Ritchie (1933-   ) was born and raised in Philadelphia and Bucks County, Pennsylvania. He joined the Air Force in 1953 during the Korean War and served one year in Waco, Texas before he was shipped to Rabat, Morocco in North Africa, where he served for the next three and one-half years. While serving in Rabat, Ron met and married a lovely French woman named Anne Marie Saunier (July 1956). Upon his honorable discharge in August 1957, the couple returned to Philadelphia, Pennsylvania where he pursued his undergraduate degree in education, and then in 1966 went on to finish his ThM degree at Dallas Theological Seminary in Dallas, Texas. Ron was called to begin full-time ministry at *Walnut Creek Presbyterian Church* in Walnut Creek, California. In 1969, he was called to join the staff at *Peninsula Bible Church* in Palo Alto, California, where he served for some 27 years with his spiritual gifts as a pastor/teacher, evangelist and visionary, and eventually in the role as an elder. In 1997, the Lord called him to join the staff of *Fellowship Bible Church* in Colorado Springs, Colorado as a pastor and elder. And then, in 2000 the Lord (in concert with a group of godly men and women) encouraged Ron to begin a non-profit organization called *Free at Last.* This ministry is designed to enable him to use his spiritual gifts of teaching, evangelism and vision within local churches, as well as to continue both his national and international conference ministry.

Ron and Anne Marie have two grown sons, Ron Jr. and Rodd. Both sons have been blessed with godly wives, Sylvia and Kyna, and both families are serving the Lord Jesus with full hearts. The Ritchie's are also now proud grandparents of five grandchildren!

You can get in touch with Ron and Anne Marie at the following address:

Free at Last

PO Box 207
Menlo Park, California 94025
email: **ritchie1st@aol.com**
www.ronritchie.com

Follow me, and I will make you fishers of men...

Jesus, Matthew 4:19, NASB

Contents

Just Show Up!

Dr. Richard C. Halverson

You go no place by accident. Wherever you go, Christ is sending you.

You are no place by mistake. Wherever you are, Christ has placed you.

You go nowhere by accident — you are nowhere by accident. Wherever you go — wherever you are— Christ is placing you or sending you, because Christ has a job He wants to do where you are and He can only do it in your body.

Think — wherever you are, Jesus Christ is literally present in the flesh. Believe that, and go in that confidence.

One of the nation's most distinguished clergymen, the Reverend Richard Christian Halverson, D.D., (1916-1995), was born in Pingree, North Dakota. He attended Valley City State Teacher College in Valley City, North Dakota before earning a Bachelor of Science degree from Wheaton College in Wheaton, Illinois. He also earned a Bachelor of Theology degree from Princeton Theological Seminary and was awarded an honorary Doctorate of Laws degree from Wheaton College. Dr. Halverson was a minister of the Presbyterian Church (USA) and served from 1958 until 1981 as the Senior Pastor of Fourth Presbyterian Church, Bethesda, Maryland. He served as the Chaplain to the U.S. Senate from February 2, 1981 until December 31, 1994. He was an Associate of the International Prayer Breakfast movement starting in 1956. He was a member of the Board of World Vision, from 1956 to 1983, serving as chairman from 1966 to 1983. He was the President of Concern Ministries, a charitable foundation in Washington, D.C..

Excerpt from **www.halverson.gospelcom.net**

Discipleship

A Four Part Series from the Gospel of Luke

Discipleship 101

How does one become a disciple of Jesus Christ?   Luke 9:18:27

    Believe Jesus is the the "Christ of God."   9:18-20
    Take up your cross daily.   9:21-23
    Be willing to lose your life.   9:24-27

Discipleship 102

Are you willing to become a disciple of Jesus Christ?   Luke 9:57-10:24

    Allow Jesus to define the calling.   9:57-62
    Allow Jesus to define the goals.   10:1-2
    Allow Jesus to define the ministry/message.   10:3-16
    Allow Jesus to evaluate your ministry.   10:17-24

Discipleship 103

Have you calculated the cost of discipleship?   Luke 14:25-35

    Be willing to hate our family   14:25
    Be willing to hate our own life   14:26
    Be willing to carry our own cross   14:27-32
    Be willing to give up all our "stuff"   14:33-35

Discipleship 104

Discipleship: A High Calling   Luke 17:1-19

    Beware of becoming a stumbling block.   17:1-2
    Be willing to rebuke/forgive a repentant brother.   17:3-4
    Ask Jesus to increase your faith.   17:5-10
    We are called to be thankful servants.   17:11-19

Discipleship

By Dietrich Bonhoeffer

*When Christ calls a man,
he bids him come and die.*

Discipleship *means adherence to Christ, and,
because Christ is the object of that adherence,
it must take the form of discipleship.*

*Christianity without the living Christ is inevitably
Christianity without discipleship, and Christianity
without discipleship is always Christianity without Christ.*

Discipleship is *"...bondage to Jesus Christ alone, completely breaking through every
program, every ideal, every set of laws. No other significance is possible, since Jesus is
the only signifcance. Besides Jesus, nothing has significance. He alone matters."*

Excerpts are taken from *The Cost of Discipleship*, © **1959 by SCM Press Ltd; First Touchstone Edition
published in 1995. Touchstone is a trademark of Simon & Schuster, New York, NY.**

HOW DO YOU BECOME A DISCIPLE OF JESUS?

Discipleship 101   Luke 9:18-27

A fellow Christian once said to me in a joking manner, "I don't mind being a servant of Jesus Christ; I just don't want to be treated like one." His words have come back to me many times as I have sought to live out my life as a follower of Jesus Christ. On occasion I find myself wanting to be a disciple of Christ, but like my friend, on my own terms.

This setting of pre-conditions for discipleship was familiar to Jesus during his ministry. He said to one man, "Follow Me," only to hear in response, "Lord, permit me first to go and bury my father." Another man told Jesus, "I will follow You, Lord; but first permit me to say good-bye to those at home" (Luke 9:57-62). True discipleship, however, has no pre-conditions. Having placed your faith in Jesus as Lord and Savior, as the apostle Paul wrote in 1 Corinthians 6:19-20: "…you are not your own…you have been bought with a price."

Dietrich Bonhoeffer, the German pastor who gave up his life daily on behalf of the German people during World War II, and who died for his faith at the end of a rope in a Nazi prison, once said, "When Christ calls a man, he bids him come and die."[1] The concept of discipleship has been greatly watered down in our modern age. From time to time it is helpful to review the true definition of discipleship as it is found in Scripture. In Luke 9:18-27 we find the answer to our question, "How does one become a disciple of Jesus Christ?"

This study is actually part of a much larger study of the entire gospel according to Luke (www.ronritchie.com). As we consider the above passage in chapter 9, I would first like to note at least eight "events" that are not mentioned in Luke's account but are reported in the other gospels, all of which take place prior to 9:18 of his gospel.

1) The Lord had first blocked the people's attempt to make him king by sending his disciples back to Capernaum by boat while he went up the mountain to pray. (Matt 14:22-23; Mk 6:45-46)

2) He joined his disciples by walking some three to four miles on the surface of the waters of Lake Galilee during a storm. You will recall that they became afraid and thought he was a ghost. Peter attempted to join him, but lost faith and almost drowned. As the Lord stepped into the boat, we read in Mark 6:51-52: "…the wind stopped; and they were greatly astonished, for they had not gained any insight from the incident of the loaves, but their heart was hardened." (Matt 14:24-33; Mk 6:47-52; Jn 6:15-21)

3) After landing in Gennesaret, Jesus continued his healing ministry. (Matt 14:34-36; Mk 6:53-56)

4) He then followed his teaching of the disciples with a discourse on the true *Bread of Life* while in the synagogue of Capernaum (John 6:22-59), which resulted in many disciples leaving him. This was followed by a confrontation with the Pharisees over the tradition of ceremonial defilement. (Matt 15:1-20; Mk 7:1-23)

5) The Lord and his disciples went northwest to the cities of Tyre and Sidon and ministered to a Gentile woman whose daughter had been possessed by demons. (Matt 15:21-28; Mk 7:24-30)

6) He returned to the eastern shores of the lake in the district of Decapolis, where the hearts of the Gentiles had been prepared by the ministry of the former demoniac named "Legion." There he healed many sick Gentiles and miraculously fed another crowd of 4,000. (Matt 15:32-39; Mk 8:1-9)

7) He returned by boat to the north coast of the Sea of Galilee, was confronted by the Pharisees, Sadducees, and Herodians, and he used that opportunity to teach his disciples "…not to beware of the leaven of bread, but of the teaching of the Pharisees and Sadducees." (Matt 16:5-12; Mk 8:13-21)

8) Finally, they returned to Bethsaida where Jesus healed a blind man, and then he and his disciples headed north to Caesarea Philippi. (Mk 8:22-26)

Jesus was in Galilee in October of the second year of his ministry. His brothers, who were not believers at the time, wanted him to go up to Jerusalem to present himself as Messiah at the Feast of Tabernacles. He didn't want to go at that time because he knew the Pharisees were seeking to kill him. His brothers eventually atended th feast and

---

[1]Dietrich Bonhoeffer, *The Cost of Discipleship,* © 1995, Touchstone; ISBN 0-6848-1500-1, paperback, 320 pages.

later Jesus would secretly attend it as well (John 5:16, 18; 7:1; 10:22-39; 19:7). But until he went up to Jerusalem, the Lord remained in northern Galilee and Decapolis gathering his true disciples around him on the slopes of Mount Hermon.

At this meeting he wanted them to clearly understand who he was and why he had to die on the cross, be buried, and be raised again on the third day. He also wanted them to know what he considered to be the marks of genuine discipleship. The future of his gospel would depend on their being faithful to follow him even unto death.

Now, as we turn to Luke 9:18-27, let this passage challenge our own commitment to Jesus Christ in our generation. Let us make sure that when we invite men and women to become disciples of our Lord, we do not present some watered-down version of what Jesus asks of his true followers. How do you become a disciple?

Believe Jesus is "The Christ of God"

Luke 9:18-20

And it happened that while He was praying alone, the disciples were with Him, and He questioned them, saying, "Who do the people say that I am?" They answered and said, "John the Baptist, and others say Elijah; but others, that one of the prophets of old has risen again." And He said to them, "But who do you say that I am?" And Peter answered and said, "The Christ of God."

Caesarea Philippi, which lies on the southern slopes of Mt. Hermon, itself being capped with snow each winter, was one of the centers of Decapolis. One of the many streams that flow through the town makes up the headwaters of the Jordan River. Through the centuries, the ancient pagans built many idols there to worship the gods. Some think that Jesus was standing on a high cliff overlooking the town which housed idols to Roman and Greek gods in its many caves and indentations when he asked this question.

We know that it was following a time of prayer when our Lord asked his disciples this important question: "In light of these gods, who do the people think I am?" (c.f. Matthew 16:13-20; Mark 8:27-30.) He was seeking to know if the people to whom the disciples had been ministering for the last year in the region of Galilee really understood who he was. Remember, the Pharisees had already denounced him as a law breaker and a Sabbath breaker, who performed all his miracles by the power of Satan. News of this would have spread quickly into every synagogue in Galilee and caused great confusion in the minds of these "sheep without a shepherd."

"John the Baptist," was the first answer Jesus received in response to his question. In Luke 19:7 we read that Herod Antipas, governor of Galilee, who had beheaded John, became perplexed when he heard of the miracles of Jesus and was told that some people thought Jesus was John the Baptist. But why would the people think that Jesus was the deceased forerunner? It was because they were looking for a Messiah who would introduce a physical kingdom. But first they would see the forerunner, as told by the prophet Malachi, who would come with a message of repentance and judgment. John and Jesus had the same message.

The disciples' second reply was that he was Elijah, the prophet and miracle worker who never died but was taken up into heaven by God some 850 years earlier, prophesied to return to earth as the forerunner of the Messiah (Malachi 4:5-6). Their third answer was that he was one of the prophets, like the miracle worker Elisha, or even Moses having been raised from the dead.

Jesus then asked the disciples a second time, "But who do *you* say that I am?" (emphasis mine). This was a very important question. Jesus was facing the cross and he needed his disciples to clearly understand his person and purpose on earth and to understand the part they would play in bringing the kingdom of God into the hearts of men and women after he returned to his Father.

All of his messages and miracles were designed so that his disciples would become fully convinced that he was the Messiah. Certainly he was not the Messiah of popular expectation. But rather, as in Isaiah 53, the man who would come to earth to suffer and die for the sins of mankind and who, on the third day, would be raised from the dead by the power of His Father.

For the Messiah to die on a cross was a stumbling block to the Jewish mind. Deuteronomy 21:22-23 states, "If a man has committed a sin worthy of death and he is put to death…he who is hanged is accursed of God…." The disciples did not understand that Jesus was about to go to the cross to become a curse for us (c.f. Galatians 3:13).

Now it was Peter's turn to answer, and by the power of spiritual revelation he answered, "The Christ of God" or as found in Matthew 16:16: "You are the Christ, the Son of the living God." In other words, Peter was saying that Jesus is the Lord's anointed as prophesied by the prophets of old. He is the promised prophet, priest and king who has come to deliver us from our sins and our enemies. John would later write of Jesus' incarnation, "And the Word became flesh, and dwelt among us, and we saw His glory, glory as of the only begotten from the Father, full of grace and truth" (John 1:14).

According to Matthew, Jesus said to Peter, "Blessed are you, Simon Barjona, because flesh and blood did not reveal this to you, but My Father who is in heaven. I also say to you that you are Peter, and upon this rock I will build My church; and the gates of Hades will not overpower it. I will give you the keys of the kingdom of heaven; and whatever you bind on earth shall have been bound in heaven, and whatever you loose on earth shall have been loosed in heaven." (Matthew 16:17-19)

Cults and worldly religions have not been given this revelation and so they continue to deny our Lord's incarnation. They say of the Lord Jesus: "Jesus is the human man and Christ is the divine ideal"; "Christ himself was nothing more than a medium high order"; "Jesus was not Jehovah God"; "Jesus is among the spirit children of Elohim, the firstborn was and is Jehovah, or Jesus Christ, to whom all others are juniors"; "Christ is considered to be one of a long line of 'masters' who had themselves realized divinity"; or, "Jesus is the Son of God, but not God the Son or God himself." But Peter was given a divine revelation from our heavenly Father as to the truth of Jesus' person: He was "The Christ of God." God incarnate!

How do you become a disciple of Jesus? You must believe in your heart that Jesus is the Christ of God, the very Son of the one and only living God—God come in the flesh. "And there is salvation in no one else; for there is no other name under heaven that has been given among men by which we must be saved" (Acts 4:12). And then, by the power of the indwelling Holy Spirit, you must…

Take up your cross daily

Luke 9:21-23

But He warned them and instructed them not to tell this to anyone, saying, "The Son of Man must suffer many things and be rejected by the elders and chief priests and scribes, and be killed and be raised up on the third day." And He was saying to them all, "If anyone wishes to come after Me, he must deny himself, and take up his cross daily and follow Me."

At this point in his ministry, Jesus warned his disciples not to tell anyone who he was because he was at the peak of his popularity with the common people. In fact, they wanted to take him by force and make him their king! Now if that happened, he would be forced to set up an earthy political kingdom and many of his followers would be unbelievers who would resist denying themselves, would not take up their cross, and would not follow him. The leaders of Israel and the majority of the Jewish people chose not to believe that he was the Son of God in spite of his person, message and miracles. Jesus wanted his disciples to be quiet about this truth until he could give his witness before the Sanhedrin in Jerusalem. At that time, the High Priest would say to him, "I adjure You by the living God, that You tell us whether You are the Christ, the Son of God" (Matthew 26:63f).

After warning them to keep quiet about who he was, Jesus prophesied concerning his own death and resurrection (9:22): "The Son of Man must suffer many things and be rejected by the elders and chief priests and scribes, and be killed and be raised up on the third day." This is the first direct prophecy our Lord gives to his disciples concerning his forthcoming suffering and death at the hands of the elders, high priest and scribes in Jerusalem. He also tells them of his physical resurrection from the dead (all these events would take place in the spring of the following year at the Passover feast). His suffering, death and resurrection were all prophesied in Isaiah 53 and Psalm 22 as God's plan to deal with the sinful fall of humanity in the Garden of Eden.

To the disciples, this "divine program" was a startling revelation. As forceful as Peter was to declare Jesus "the Christ of God," he was just as ready to rebuke the Lord and his plans. Matthew 16:22-23 records Peter as saying, "God forbid it, Lord! This shall never happen to You." But [Jesus] turned and said to Peter, "Get behind Me, Satan! You are a stumbling block to Me; for you are not setting your mind on *God's interests*, but man's" (emphasis mine).

"God's interests" had already been prophesied by the prophet Isaiah:

He was despised and forsaken of men,
    A man of sorrows and acquainted with grief;
And like one from whom men hide their face
    He was despised, and we did not esteem Him.
Surely our griefs He Himself bore,
    And our sorrows He carried;
Yet we ourselves esteemed Him stricken,
    Smitten of God, and afflicted.
But He was pierced through for our transgressions,
    He was crushed for our iniquities;
The chastening for our well-being fell upon Him,
    And by His scourging we are healed.
All of us like sheep have gone astray,
    Each of us has turned to his own way;
But the LORD has caused the iniquity of us all
    to fall on Him. (Isaiah 53:3-6)

Once we place our faith in Jesus as Lord and Savior we become his bondservant and we begin to learn to live our lives to fulfill his will, not ours. We will need to deny our self-confidence, our self-adequacy, as well as our self-sufficiency. C.E.B Canfield once said, *"To deny oneself means to choose by the power of the Holy Spirit to live daily in the spiritual reality that Paul shared with the Corinthians, 'You are not your own; you have been bought with a price' (1 Corinthians 6:19-20). To deny oneself...is to turn away from the idolatry of self-centeredness."* Either Jesus is Lord of our lives or we are. We cannot have it both ways so the key attitude of our new lives in Christ is stated in the words of our Lord the night before he died on the cross for our sins: "Father, if You are willing, remove this cup from Me; yet not My will, but Yours be done" (Luke 22:42).

Jesus followed up his prophecy by saying that if after confessing him as Messiah one still wants to follow him, "he must deny himself, and take up his cross daily..." The Roman cross was an instrument of shame, humiliation and death and was used by the government to punish criminals. When the Jews watched a criminal take up a cross and be led by a squad of Roman soldiers to the hill of Calvary, they all knew the man was making a one-way trip to his death. The criminal takes up his cross under duress, but the Christian does it willingly, by the power of the Holy Spirit.

Taking up my cross means that I admit it was for my sin of envy, rebellion, pride, lust, murder, adultery, slander, etc. that Jesus died on that cross. However, once I placed my faith in him, I died once and for all to the power of sin. And now, because he lives, I am able to live a new, resurrected life of righteousness by his resurrection power (c.f. Romans 6). The cross of Christ is a daily reminder that our flesh needs to be put to death. The apostle Paul said years later to the Galatians, "Now those who belong to Christ Jesus have crucified the flesh with its passions and desires. If we live by the Spirit, let us also walk by the Spirit" (Galatians 5:24-25).

We are not to coddle or cuddle our flesh, nor give it any encouragement or even tolerate it. Instead we are to reject it altogether with its selfish desires. We are to nail "the flesh" to the cross daily. Paul tells us that if Jesus is Lord, then "...we who live are constantly being delivered over to death for Jesus' sake, so that the life of Jesus also may be manifested in our mortal flesh. So death works in us, but life in you" (2 Corinthians 4:11-12). In his book, *The Cross of Christ*, John R.W. Stott wrote, *"The cross undermines our self-righteousness. We stand before it with a bowed head and a broken spirit, and there we remain until the Lord Jesus speaks to our hearts his word of pardon and acceptance, and we, gripped by his love and brimful of thanksgiving, go out into the world to live our lives in his service."[2]*

There were many disciples who were willing to follow Jesus for a while, but then they would leave him because he continued to offer them a spiritual kingdom when what they really wanted was a political kingdom. Yet, the offer of the Lord was that *true* disciples would not only deny themselves and take up their cross, but would also "follow him" wherever he led them, even if it was to their own physical death on a cross (the same death Peter would suffer at the end of his life). The disciples were asked to trust the Lord as "he set his face toward Jerusalem" (Luke 9:51, ASV) to suffer, die and be raised again. So, to follow Jesus means to walk in obedience to his word so that our lives bring glory to him and joy to our own hearts.

Most of us have seen the movie *Chariots of Fire*, a true story about two outstanding athletes who participated in the 1924 Olympic Games held in Paris, France. One of the athletes was Eric Liddell, a Scotsman and a Christian who won the gold medal and set a world record in the 400 meter race. Following the Games, Eric was called of God to serve as a missionary in China. When the Japanese invaded China in the 1930s, Eric's task of teaching and his ministry of evangelism in the countryside brought him face to face with the victims of that war. On several occasions he was called upon to rescue wounded and dying men who were left untreated because the local people feared reprisals from the Japanese.

Just before the bombing of Pearl Harbor, Eric was rounded up with all of the other "enemy nationals" and was placed in a prison camp. There he taught the other prisoners, including children, the Word of God, and he also tried to help with their medical needs. He died at the age of 43, just months before the liberation, and was buried in a little cemetery in the Japanese part of the camp. Do you remember the last lines that came up on screen at the end of the movie? "ERIC LIDDELL. MISSIONARY. DIED IN OCCUPIED CHINA AT THE END OF WORLD WAR II. ALL SCOTLAND MOURNED."

How do you become a disciple of Jesus? You must believe that he is the Christ; take up your cross daily, and you must...

Be willing to lose your life

Luke 9:24-27

For whoever wishes to save his life will lose it, but whoever loses his life for My sake, he is the one who will save it. For what is a man profited if he gains the whole world, and loses or forfeits himself? For whoever is ashamed of Me and My words, the Son of Man will be ashamed of him when He comes in His glory, and the glory of the Father and of the holy angels. But I say to you truthfully, there are some of those standing here who

---

[2]John R.W. Stott, *The Cross of Christ,* © 1986, InterVarsity Press; ISBN 0-877-84998-6, paperback, 383 pages.

will not taste death until they see the kingdom of God.

The disciples were aware that John the Baptist had "lost" his life daily from the time he was a youth, up until the time of his physical death at the hands of Herod and Herodias. During the next 30 years, 11 of the 12 disciples would be placed into circumstances in which they would have to daily give up their hopes and dreams in order to remain faithful to their Lord and to their calling as his apostles. They would be persecuted, arrested, tried, placed in prisons, beaten, suffer cold, hunger, loneliness, fear and abandonment, all for the sake of Christ. And in the end, all but perhaps John would die a martyr's death. "Remember the word that I said to you," Jesus said to them in the upper room. "A slave is not greater than his master. If they persecuted Me, they will also persecute you…" (John 15:20). Paul would tell his spiritual son, Timothy, some 30 years later that, "…all who desire to live godly in Christ Jesus will be persecuted" (2 Timothy 3:12). The writer to the Hebrews reminded the Christian community that they would be made a public spectacle through reproaches and tribulations, partly by becoming sharers with those who were so treated: "For you showed sympathy to the prisoners, and accepted joyfully the seizure of your property, knowing that you have for yourselves a better possession and an abiding one [in eternity]" (Hebrews 10:32-35).

Jesus had preached earlier that he was the Bread of Life, and everyone who believed in him would be given the gift of eternal life: "'It is the Spirit who gives life; the flesh profits nothing; the words that I have spoken to you are spirit and are life. But there are some of you who do not believe.' For Jesus knew from the beginning who they were who did not believe, and who it was that would betray Him…As a result of this many of His disciples withdrew and were not walking with Him anymore" (John 6:63-64, 66).

That statement, "But there are some of you who do not believe," may have been directed at Judas who was having second thoughts about the person and claims of Jesus. Judas was a Jewish Zealot before he met Jesus. He had hoped that the Lord would set up a powerful political kingdom that would overthrow the Roman government. But the more he listened to the Lord, the more it became apparent that Jesus was speaking of a spiritual kingdom. Judas was not about to lose his life for a man he really didn't believe was the "political" Messiah he had hoped would save Israel from Roman domination. Thus, he took steps to save his own life but in doing so, actually lost it.

"For what does it profit a man to gain the whole world, and forfeit his soul? For what will a man give in exchange for his soul?" (Mark 8:36-37). Where are you investing your life? Remember the words of Satan at the beginning of Jesus' ministry? "Again, the devil took Him to a very high mountain and showed Him all the kingdoms of the world and their glory; and he said to Him, 'All these things I will give You, if You fall down and worship me'" (Matthew 4:8-9). The Roman Caesars thought they had approached this high watermark when they were declared to be the gods of Rome and Emperors of the world. Yet each died in their turn and took into eternity all that they were born with—nothing but their soul! The man who built his life on a sandy foundation lost his house, his life, and his soul when the deadly storm finally hit. This would be true of Herod Antipas, the High Priest, the Pharisees, Sadducees and scribes, and finally, Judas—all of whom thought this world was all there was and invested so heavily in it that they lost their souls.

"For whoever is ashamed of Me and My words in this adulterous and sinful generation, the Son of Man will also be ashamed of him when He comes in the glory of His Father with the holy angels" (Mark 8:38). Matthew adds, quoting Psalm 62:12 and Proverbs 24:12, "For the Son of Man is going to come in the glory of His Father with His angels, and WILL THEN REPAY EVERY MAN ACCORDING TO HIS DEEDS" (Matthew 16:27). Here our Lord is speaking of his second coming—after his death, resurrection and ascension—because he makes reference to the great white throne of judgment, in which all the deeds of men will be weighed and found wanting. Paul reminded the Ephesians, "For by grace you have been saved through faith; and that not of yourselves, it is the gift of God; not as a result of works, so that no one may boast" (2:8-9).

"But I say to you truthfully, there are some of those standing here who will not taste death until they see the kingdom of God" (Luke 9:27). Matthew adds, "…until they see the Son of Man coming in His kingdom" (16:28). Mark says, "…until they see the kingdom of God after it has come with power" (9:1).[3] None of this glory will be stopped by the rejection of the Pharisees, the High Priest, the Supreme Court, the political powers of Rome, or even our Lord's death on the cross.

How do you become a disciple of Jesus? Believe he is "the Christ of God" then take up your cross daily and be willing to lose your life!

---

[3]In the immediate context it appears that our Lord is referring to the time eight days later, when he will take his disciples out of Caesarea Philippi and move higher up the slopes of Mt. Hermon. There, Peter, James and John would see the Transfiguration of Jesus and be allowed to look into eternity and see the risen Savior in all his glory and power. This is the vision all the world will finally see at his second coming when he assumes his rightful position as King of kings and Lord of lords. (Luke 9:30-36)

The Great Need for

Making Disciples

By John R. W. Stott

The numbers of people coming to Christ around the world
are staggering. Today we are witnessing perhaps one of the
greatest expansions of the Church worldwide, especially in
the Two-Thirds World. These numbers would suggest great
success stories--that the mission of the Church is being
accomplished.

And yet, very reputable and deeply committed church
leaders from Two-Thirds World countries are quick to note that the Church is exploding with
extra-ordinary numerical growth *without depth*. We are witnessing one of the most *over-
evangelized*, but *under-discipled* eras in history.

The Research and Development of the Church, "In The Gap" published by John Stott Ministries, December
2002 issue, p. 1.

In 1950, John R. W. Stott became the rector of All Souls Church, which is located in London, England. In
1975 he became Rector Emeritus, and then he began *John R. W. Stott Ministries*. Out of JSM, Stott has
blessed the world with his gifts of pastor-teacher, evangelist, and preacher. He is both a scholar and Christian
statesman, and is committed to discipling young people within third-world communities.

ARE YOU WILLING TO BECOME A DISCIPLE OF JESUS?

Discipleship 102   Luke 9:57-10:24

In the beginning of our Lord's ministry, he said to a few fishermen sitting in their boats, as well a few of those fixing their nets by the shore of Lake Galilee, "Follow Me, and I will make you become fishers of men" (Mark 1:17). We are told that Peter and Andrew, along with James and John, *immediately* left their nets and followed him. They were later joined by eight other men, and together, over the next three years, they did indeed become fishers of men. They went through a process of being discipled by the Lord, learning to live *for* him and *with* him, in order to take the good news of salvation into their generation and the generations to come. Jesus then went to the cross and took upon himself the sins of all mankind, died and was buried. After three days, God the Father raised him from the grave. He appeared to his disciples over the next 40 days, and then just before he was to ascend back into the presence of his Father he gathered his eleven disciples and said:

"All authority has been given to Me in heaven and on earth. Go therefore and make disciples of all the nations, baptizing them in the name of the Father and the Son and the Holy Spirit, teaching them to observe all that I commanded you; and lo, I am with you always, even to the end of the age." (Matthew 18:18-20)

Some 20 years later, a second-generation Christian and disciple named Paul would share the goal of discipleship with the Colossians. He wrote that he was delighted to reveal the mystery of God to the Gentiles, "which is Christ in you, the hope of glory. We proclaim Him, admonishing every man and teaching every man with all wisdom, so that we may present every man complete in Christ" (Colossians 1:27-28). In other words, "maturity" is the goal—being totally set free from dependence on self and becoming dependent on God; being ruled not by circumstances but by the sovereign God, Jesus.

In the summer of AD 67, the apostle Paul, having served the Lord Jesus faithfully for some 30 years, was spending his last days on earth in a Roman prison awaiting his death by beheading. Never being one to bemoan his circumstances, he wrote the following words of encouragement to his spiritual son and faithful disciple Timothy (of the next generation of believers):

"You therefore, my son, be strong in the grace that is in Christ Jesus. The things which you have heard from me in the presence of many witnesses, entrust these to faithful men who will be able to teach others also. Suffer hardship with me, as a good soldier of Christ Jesus." (2 Timothy 2:1-3)

Paul lived out his life in obedience to the command of his risen Lord; a command spoken some 35 years earlier.

The apostles, as well as Paul's disciples, were faithful in their generation to their calling, and all the generations to follow have been faithful to their calling, to one degree or another. The fruit is seen in the lives of the maturing Christians by whom we are both surrounded and encouraged. In this modern era, particularly in our western society, the church of Jesus Christ is struggling with the whole concept of discipleship. There are so many voices calling out for our time and energy, many of us find ourselves losing the spiritual wisdom to come before the Lord for our focus. Our Lord has called us to put time aside to have a relationship with him and to invest in the spiritual maturity of younger believers.

The temptation for the church, because of the lack of time and energy, is to invest money in packaged, self-improvement programs which are supposedly designed to produce mature men and women for Christ in the privacy of their own homes, sometimes in as little as 12 weeks! The fruit of such programs is contained in a 3-ring binder that eventually just sits on a shelf in our home libraries. But we need to understand that our Lord's command still stands for each generation until he comes again: "Go therefore and make disciples of all the nations." When he comes again he should find his faithful followers either discipling others in this generation, or being discipled themselves by mature believers.

As we turn to Luke 9:57-10:24, we realize that our risen Lord is still calling men and women today. For once Jesus becomes our Lord and Savior he expects us to not only follow him, but to be available to be discipled by him through both his Word and in relationships with mature believers. That way his heart of love and his message of salvation will be taken into the next generation—the discipled become the disciplers—bearing in mind that this is a process that takes a lifetime. The question we want to ask ourselves today is, "Are you willing to become a disciple of Jesus Christ?" If so,

Allow Jesus to define the calling

At this point in our study of Luke's gospel account, our Lord had been ministering in northern Galilee, and then he had moved south to the city of Capernaum where he healed a demoniac boy. He then determined to "…set his face toward Jerusalem" (Luke 9:51, ASV). As he traveled south toward the holy city, the shadow of the cross fell heavily across his path, and his heart was burdened with the reality that "He came to His own, and those who were His own did not receive Him" (John 1:11). But he was also burdened with the reality that the sheep of Israel had no Shepherd. During those last few months before the cross, our Lord spent more and more time with his disciples—teaching them to bring his gospel of the kingdom into the age of the Spirit after his resurrection. But the twelve disciples who had been with Jesus for the last two and a half years were still struggling to understand all the spiritual principles of discipleship within the spiritual kingdom of God.

In Luke 9:52-56, for example, Jesus wanted his disciples to go ahead and set up some sleeping arrangements at a Samaritan village for the group. The Jews and the Samaritans (a mixed race of Jews and Gentiles) were not on the best of terms because of a rebuke by the prophet Ezra some 400 years earlier concerning mixed marriages. So when a Samaritan innkeeper heard that Jesus and his men were heading south to worship in Jerusalem instead of worshiping on Mount Gerizim, he responded, "No way, José!" and refused to receive them. As a result, the brothers James and John, whom Jesus called the "Sons of Thunder" (Mark 3:17), asked the Lord if they could destroy the village with fire as Elijah had done 850 years earlier to the Baal priest on Mount Carmel.

It seems they had lost track of the whole point of Jesus' ministry, and Luke tells us in 9:55-56, "But He turned and rebuked them, [and said, 'You do not know what kind of spirit you are of; for the Son of Man did not come to destroy men's lives, but to save them']." John wrote, in his gospel: "For God so loved the world, that He gave His only begotten Son, that whoever believes in Him shall not perish, but have eternal life" (3:16).

At the same time, of course, our Lord was aware of the need to train more men and women from among the local crowds who sincerely wanted to follow him and proclaim his message of salvation while he was still alive on earth, and even following after his death, resurrection and ascension. They would have to be trained in such a way that they would be able to not only proclaim the gospel in their own generation, but to disciple future generations until he returned to this earth as King of kings and Lord of lords.

Luke 9:57-62

As they were going along the road, someone said to Him, "I will follow You wherever You go." And Jesus said to him, "The foxes have holes and the birds of the air have nests, but the Son of Man has nowhere to lay His head." And He said to another, "Follow Me." But he said, "Lord, permit me first to go and bury my father." But He said to him, "Allow the dead to bury their own dead; but as for you, go and proclaim everywhere the kingdom of God." Another also said, "I will follow You, Lord; but first permit me to say good-bye to those at home." But Jesus said to him, "No one, after putting his hand to the plow and looking back, is fit for the kingdom of God."

Basically, we are called to *lose* our lives. In Luke 9:18-27, we found our Lord teaching his twelve disciples just what he considered to be the true marks of a genuine follower. The men and women who desire to follow him must: 1) Believe that he is "the Christ of God" (9:18-20); 2) Be willing to take up their cross and die daily (9:21-23)—die to their hopes, dreams, and ambitions; and eventually, should the situation call for it, 3) Be willing to lose their life as Jesus' cousin John the Baptist had under the wicked hand of Herod Antipas (9:24-27). For when God calls a man or woman to follow him he calls them to die so that he can live his life in and through them. In other words, we are called to leave our "comfort zones."

As Jesus was traveling with his twelve men in Galilee, three other men who were apparently part of an amazed and admiring crowd, each in turn approached him hoping to also become one of his disciples.

The first man said, "I will follow you anywhere!" But Jesus said to him, "The foxes have holes and the birds of the air have nests, but the Son of Man has nowhere to lay His head." Jesus response causes us to wonder if this man really understood what it meant to follow the Lord Jesus Christ. He would be called to live like our Lord—moving from village to village, house to house, cave to cave, etc. without any hope of having a place he could call home. For since the beginning of our Lord's life in Bethlehem, "there was no room…in the inn" (Luke 2:7).

As an adult Jesus had been forced out of his home town of Nazareth. Later, the leaders of Jerusalem and the people of Judea and Galilee had rejected him, and most recently the Samaritan innkeeper had refused to give him lodging. So would this potential disciple be truly willing to follow

Jesus anywhere and give up all the comfort and security of home and family? Apparently not for we don't ever hear of him again.

Luke then tells us that "[Jesus] said to another, 'Follow Me.' But he said, "Lord, permit me first to go and bury my father.'" This man not only felt an obligation to bury his father, but to also observe the 30-day mourning period which was a duty and a sign of kindness. But the call to discipleship had to be accepted when issued or it would be lost. As for his dead father, there were enough people who were still spiritually dead to handle the burial and so Jesus says further to the second man: "Allow the dead to bury their own dead; but as for you, go and proclaim everywhere the kingdom of God."

This man seemed to be willing to follow the Lord, but he wanted to set the agenda (the terms) of discipleship. Jesus responded by challenging his loyalties and his deeper motives for wanting to be a disciple. If Jesus is the sovereign Lord, then following him means obeying his commandments without conditions or reservation.

A third man said, "I will follow You, Lord; but first permit me to say goodbye to those at home." But Jesus said to him, "No one, after putting his hand to the plow and looking back, is fit for the kingdom of God." Once again we see that our Lord was able to read the motives of this man's heart. He knew that if this man went back to his family, they might prevail on him in a variety of ways—perhaps the obligation to a family business or other loyalties. So that even if he eventually did follow the Lord, in time he could drop out, filled with guilt that he wasn't providing for his family. This man had a divided heart.

The Lord, knowing our hearts so well, would hear Peter say later: "Behold, we have left everything and followed You" and Jesus responded, "Truly I say to you, there is no one who has left house or brothers or sisters or mother or father or children or farms, for My sake and for the gospel's sake, but that he will receive a hundred times as much now in the present age, houses and brothers and sisters and mothers and children and farms, along with persecutions; and in the age to come, eternal life." (Mark 10:28-30)

One of the most cherished privileges the people and staff have been given at Peninsula Bible Church is the encouragement by the elders to invest our lives in discipling men and women. The spiritual principles we use are all the same, though the method of each one differs to fit a variety of personalities. Yet the spiritual fruit is all the same—a deep and abiding joy in our hearts as we watch our disciples grow into spiritual maturity and begin discipling others.

Steve Zeisler, a pastor at PBC, was telling us of the joy of taking 15 men in his Thursday morning study to Mexico to help finish the construction of a church. As he was shar-ing his experiences of living, eating, and working with those men, the joy in his eyes and spirit must have been similar to Noah's joy when he parked his ark on Mount Ararat! And again, one of the PBC elders, Ed Woodhall, who had been discipling some young married couples, called me just to tell me the joy he was having in investing his life in these couples—sharing his biblical knowledge and spiritual experiences with them. They had arrived at a point in their lives where they wanted to begin to disciple others, and were doing so! On and on it goes, faithful men and women among us willing to be discipled and then to disciple others in return until the Lord comes back.

Are you willing to become a disciple of Jesus Christ? Allow him to define the calling, and then…

Allow Jesus to define the goals

Luke 10:1-2

Now after this the Lord appointed seventy others, and sent them in pairs ahead of Him to every city and place where He Himself was going to come. And He was saying to them, "The harvest is plentiful, but the laborers are few; therefore beseech the Lord of the harvest to send out laborers into His harvest."

It is at this point, according to John 7-8, that our Lord arrived in Jerusalem to celebrate the Feast of Tabernacles (or Booths) some time in October, and he began to teach in the temple. In response to his teaching, some of the religious leaders said he had a demon, while others rejected him as Messiah. Even so, of the multitude following him, many believed in him. The Pharisees sought to arrest him, but Jesus hid himself and went out of the temple, returning to Galilee (John 8:59).

Jesus had already sent out his twelve disciples (as recorded in Luke 9:1-10) to minister in Galilee and now, out of the many that were following him on a daily basis, he chose some 70 new disciples. Their assignment was to travel in pairs and minister in the cities and countryside of Jordan and Judea and prepare Israel for the official offer of her King. (The triumphal entry into Jerusalem was only a few months away.) Once they had opened the doors to these people, Jesus would follow behind them and minister to them.

The goal of our Lord's ministry was well-stated in Luke 19:10: "For the Son of Man has come to seek and to save that which was lost." The goal of our Lord's ministry must also be the goal of our ministry: the salvation of the spiritually lost in every city, village, farm, home, and country, and in every generation until he comes again (see Matthew 28:18-20). Our Lord encouraged these new disciples with words of great joy when he said that "the harvest was plentiful."

There were many men, women, and children who were ready to enter the kingdom of God because the salvation process had already been started by the Lord; he had cast the Word of God on good soil, and that seed had grown to the point that all that was left to do was to go into the fields and harvest those willing hearts. So many, in fact, that the Lord showed them that they would be overwhelmed by seeing the fields so full with grain ready for harvest, perhaps realizing that there were so few workers to harvest the grain. But rather than panic, they were to pray; to "beseech the Lord of the harvest to send out [more] laborers."

During the first week of October 1990, Anne Marie and I visited our friends Dudley and Janet Wiener who were, at that time, living and ministering as missionaries in Paris. Dudley was first discipled by Jeff Farrar (who was discipled by Steve Zeisler and me a few years earlier, and then eventually went on to become the pastor at Central Peninsula Church in Foster City, California). Dudley was later discipled in PBC's intern program, as well as by the pastors involved with *Careers Alive* (a "singles" ministry) and the Sunday evening *Body Life* services.

Dudley felt called by God to go to Paris, and over the next few years saw God open doors through which he and his family could minister, as directed by an evangelical mission board. As I walked through the streets of Paris with Dudley one day, I felt the spiritual pressure of living in a city of 12 million people of many different races, philosophies, and religions. It can give you a real feeling of helplessness. How in the world do you penetrate such spiritual darkness with the gospel of Jesus Christ? But when I shared this feeling with Dudley, his response was, "Why don't we pray?" So again, we are to be encouraged by the words of our Lord: "The harvest is plentiful, but the laborers are few; therefore beseech the Lord of the harvest to send out laborers into His harvest."

Are you willing to become a disciple of Jesus Christ? Then allow Jesus to define the calling and the goal, and then…

Allow Jesus define the ministry/message

Luke 10:3-16

"Go; behold, I send you out as lambs in the midst of wolves. Carry no money belt, no bag, no shoes; and greet no one on the way. Whatever house you enter, first say, 'Peace be to this house.' If a man of peace is there, your peace will rest on him; but

if not, it will return to you. Stay in that house, eating and drinking what they give you; for the laborer is worthy of his wages. Do not keep moving from house to house. Whatever city you enter and they receive you, eat what is set before you; and heal those in it who are sick, and say to them, 'The kingdom of God has come near to you.' But whatever city you enter and they do not receive you, go out into its streets and say, 'Even the dust of your city which clings to our feet we wipe off in protest against you; yet be sure of this, that the kingdom of God has come near.' I say to you, it will be more tolerable in that day for Sodom than for that city.

Woe to you, Chorazin! Woe to you, Bethsaida! For if the miracles had been performed in Tyre and Sidon which occurred in you, they would have repented long ago, sitting in sackcloth and ashes. But it will be more tolerable for Tyre and Sidon in the judgment than for you. And you, Capernaum, will not be exalted to heaven, will you? You will be brought down to Hades! The one who listens to you listens to Me, and the one who rejects you rejects Me; and he who rejects Me rejects the One who sent Me."

Here we see our Lord giving his 70 new disciples the same kind of instruction he gave the twelve earlier: 1) They need to know that they are going into enemy territory, as lambs among hungry wolves; 2) They are to make no provision for the next day, but trust God for each day of ministry; 3) They are not to allow themselves to become sidetracked, but they are to pick a city and focus on it; and, 4) Once they arrive at a city, they are to find a home that would respond to their peaceful greeting, and if invited, to come in and stay the whole time, eating and drinking without complaint whatever was put before them.

Further, they are to prepare the people for the gospel message by healing those who are sick and preaching, "The kingdom of God has come near to you." That is, God's sovereign rule was about to enter their hearts when the Lord Jesus came, and they would experience their complete salvation.

But Jesus also instructed these disciples to give a word of judgment to the cities that would not receive them. They were to go out into the street, take off their sandals and shake off the dust in protest. Then they were to give them a warning: "The kingdom of God has come near." In rejecting the disciples these people would have, in truth, also rejected their Messiah. Yet, the kingdom would not be stopped from coming, even if they tried to ignore it.

Christ then gave his personal word of judgment. As there are different degrees of glory for the saints, so we can see that there are different degrees of judgment that our Lord will pass out on the day of final judgment to those who have rejected him, his message, and his messengers. The judgment will be based on the amount of spiritual light they received and then rejected while living on earth. As these cities were given more truth, along with it they were given more responsibility to receive it. The message these cities were given was so great that if they turned it down, woe to them!

Sodom, the city of Abraham's and Lot's day, was physically judged by fire because of its wickedness against the Lord. "Sodom and Gomorrah…indulged in gross immorality and went after strange flesh…" (Jude, verse 7). But any city that was given the offer of salvation by the Messiah's disciples, and then rejected it, would be judged more severely than Sodom of old.

Chorazin and Bethsaida were located close to Capernaum, so Jesus must have visited them many times, preaching the kingdom of God and doing signs and wonders. Then the Lord told his disciples to tell the cities that rejected him, "For if the miracles had been performed in Tyre and Sidon which occurred in you, they would have repented long ago, sitting in sackcloth and ashes. But it will be more tolerable for Tyre and Sidon in the judgment than for you."

The prophet Amos denounced these Phoenician cities around 780 B.C. for selling the Jews as slaves to the Edomites and then the prophet Joel, in the same century, denounced them for selling the Jewish children to the Greeks. Capernaum was the port city our Lord called home. It was where he worshipped, where he chose some of his early disciples, where he performed many miracles and wonders, and where he spoke many times to the crowd about his Person and purpose. But after all was said and done, except for a few disciples, the crowd dropped off and rejected his Messiah-ship. "And you, Capernaum, will not be exalted to heaven, will you? You will be brought down to Hades [the place of torment and flame]!" (See also Luke 16:23-24.) That city is now laid in ruins.

The disciples were sent out to a variety of cities and villages to proclaim the good news of salvation, which could only be found in Jesus. Most of us are not called to preach to a whole city or village but to individuals. Yet the spiritual principle remains the same: "The one who listens to you listens to Me, and the one who rejects you rejects Me; and he who rejects Me rejects the One who sent Me" (Luke 10:16). Woe to those who reject the Lord Jesus and his offer of salvation for the day of judgment is coming.

I thought of that verse when I officiated at a wedding of a Christian couple. One set of parents were not Christians and the wedding ceremony was offensive to their secular beliefs. After the ceremony, the wedding party and guests were invited to this couple's home for a reception. When I arrived a few minutes later than most of the guests, I saw the parents standing at the front door welcoming someone just ahead of me and I walked up with a joyful heart hoping to greet them. As I approached, the woman saw me and said, "Excuse me, we are very busy!" and slammed the door in my face. This verse flashed across my mind as my heart wept for them. It occurred to me that they were still living in their sin and darkness and Jesus said, "…the one who rejects you rejects Me; and he who rejects Me rejects the One who sent Me."

Are you willing to become a disciple of Jesus Christ? Then allow Jesus to define the calling, the goals, and the ministry and message, and then…

Allow Jesus to evaluate your ministry

Luke 10:17-24

The seventy returned with joy, saying, "Lord, even the demons are subject to us in Your name." And He said to them, "I was watching Satan fall from heaven like lightning. Behold, I have given you authority to tread on serpents and scorpions, and over all the power of the enemy, and nothing will injure you. Nevertheless do not rejoice in this, that the spirits are subject to you, but rejoice that your names are recorded in heaven."

At that very time He rejoiced greatly in the Holy Spirit, and said, "I praise You, O Father, Lord of heaven and earth, that You have hidden these things from the wise and intelligent and have revealed them to infants. Yes, Father, for this way was well-pleasing in Your sight. All things have been handed over to Me by My Father, and no one knows who the Son is except the Father, and who the Father is except the Son, and anyone to whom the Son wills to reveal Him."

Turning to the disciples, He said privately, "Blessed are the eyes which see the things you see, for I say to you, that many prophets and kings wished to see the things which you see, and did not see them, and to hear the things which you hear, and did not hear them."

Those 70 men returned to the Lord and it soon became obvious that they had walked in obedience to his instructions. As a result, they returned to be evaluated just as the twelve disciples before them (c.f. Luke 9:10). They were very much like many of us who are given ministries by the Lord. When we return from Columbia, Mexico, Romania, France, Java, Timor or wherever the Lord has sent us, we are usually very excited about what the Lord did in and through us.

And so were the disciples: "Lord, even the demons are subject to us in Your name." Jesus responded, "I was watching Satan fall from heaven like lightning." In the immediate context it seems that what Jesus was saying was, "You were experiencing my power at work in and through you so you could cast out demons while on earth, but I want you to know that I was present when Satan was cast out of heaven. His power was broken then, it was broken at my temptation in the wilderness, it is broken now by my power through you, and as I look into eternity, his power will be broken in the future by all who deal with him and his demons in my name."

He continued, "I have given you authority to tread upon serpents and scorpions, and over all the power of the enemy, and nothing shall injure you [I will protect you from attacks by Satan—he's a murderer who wants to kill you]. Nevertheless, do not rejoice in this, that the spirits are subject to you, but rejoice that your names are recorded in heaven." What Jesus means is, don't rejoice in the activities of a ministry because these works were set out beforehand for us, and all we have to do is walk in them. We are to rejoice in the fact that we have an eternal relationship with the living God (c.f. Ephesian 2:10).

As our Lord listened to the many wonderful reports of his disciples, he rushed into the presence of his Father rejoicing greatly. "Father, you are awesome!" for the Holy Spirit had provided the power and protection for his men. He praised his Father, Lord of heaven and earth (and Lord over Satan), because he had worked these mighty works through his spiritual babes, rather than through the seemingly wise and intelligent (or the priestly class in Jerusalem), and this was all pleasing in his Father's sight. Did you ever think that Jesus is rejoicing like that over your life as you seek to walk in obedience to him? He is! And he rejoices that the gift of salvation has been given to him by his Father to reveal to whomever he desires.

The Lord reminded his disciples of their many spiritual blessings. They needed to understand that they had been blessed more than the prophets and kings of old, who had wished to see the glory and power of the Messiah and to hear the wonderful message of redemption being preached to the people of Israel. They had watched generation after generation of male children born in Bethlehem, wondering about each one, "Is this the one?" The disciples were not kings like David or prophets like Moses and Elijah or Isaiah and Jeremiah—all who had looked forward to the fulfillment of this day. But they really got to see, hear, and experience it. "I am He!" Jesus was saying. And because they were only spiritual babes he wanted them to take in the blessing of his Father, the blessing that was right in front of them.

If you are willing to become a disciple of Jesus Christ, you must then allow him to define the calling, to define the goals, to define the message and ministry, and to evaluate that ministry. As a result of this wonderful relationship with the Lord as the Son of God, and your willingness to be a disciple of Jesus Christ, you can then:

- Rejoice that your names are recorded in heaven!
- Rejoice that the Lord uses you to minister in his harvest!
- Rejoice that you are privileged to see truth in this generation that those faithful men of old longed to see but never did!

Every one of us who have come into a relationship with Jesus Christ should ask the Lord to move our hearts to be willing to be discipled. Those of us who have been walking with the Lord for awhile need to be discipling others, teaching them the truth of God, the principles of the ministry, teaching them how to walk by faith, teaching them about their spiritual gifts, and teaching the younger ones as they come along. All of us should be in a discipling mode—either receiving or giving—and always continuing toward maturity ourselves. For example, I'm always listening to other Bible teachers, seeking to learn from them and grow in maturity in Christ.

I've been walking with the Lord for over 45 years and I feel like a child when it comes to the mysteries of the kingdom of God! I'm always hungry for more. You should have the same heart, which is given by the Holy Spirit. Are you willing to be discipled? Are you willing to allow the Lord to take your life without conditions and without trying to set the agenda? I hope so! Follow after Jesus, and he will make you to become fishers of men.

HAVE YOU CALCULATED THE COST OF BECOMING A DISCIPLE OF JESUS?

Discipleship 103   Luke 14:25-35

A long time ago I received a letter from Dudley Weiner, a pastor and evangelist, who was serving our Lord in Paris, France at the time. Dudley (previously an intern at PBC) took his wife Janet and their three children on vacation one summer to the seaport town of St. Jean de Luz in the southwest of France. In his letter he talked about a walk he took along the beach with a young man and a conversation they had.

I seemed to be aware of each step into the soft sand as I purposely strode along the narrow strip of beach, laden with sun bathers. My mind raced with images from the past and questions for the present as I looked at the young man next to me...We sat down in the balmy sand. As I looked into his eyes and he looked back into mine, I saw innocence and sincerity and at the same time determination and certitude. I said, "Are you sure you want to do this?" He affirmed, "Yes." I continued, "You must first understand the cost of this decision and how it will affect the rest of your life." He listened patiently. I said, "It's not something you can take lightly. It will stand out as a landmark decision in your life. God will honor this decision and so will I...It means you want to be a follower of Jesus Christ and truly be his disciple." He affirmed, "Yes."

Two thousand years ago our Lord Jesus had a similar experience with two brothers named Peter and Andrew on the sandy shores of the Sea of Galilee. They were fisherman, engaged in casting their nets into the sea when he came along. He called out to them, "Follow Me, and I will make you become fishers of men. And they immediately left their nets and followed Him" (Mark 1:16-20). Over the past two thousand years, Jesus has continued to call out men and women from this fallen world to follow him. If we decide to leave our nets and go, he leads us through the door of "Discipleship University." Within its hallowed halls he begins to introduce us to a prescribed set of spiritual courses that will enable us, over the process of time, to disciple others in our generation.

As we considered chapter 9 of Luke's gospel (Discipleship 101), we found our Lord talking to his disciples at Caesarea Philippi. There, at the headwaters of the Jordan River, he spoke to them about the cost of discipleship saying:

"The Son of Man must suffer many things and be rejected by the elders and chief priests and scribes, and be killed and be raised up on the third day." And He was saying to them all, "If anyone wishes to come after Me, he must deny himself, and take up his cross daily and follow Me."

"For whoever wishes to save his life will lose it, but whoever loses his life for My sake, he is the one who will save it. For what is a man profited if he gains the whole world, and loses or forfeits himself?" (9:21-25).

In other words, there is a cost to discipleship. Christian discipleship is not like joining the Elks or the Boy Scouts of America. Following Jesus may result in losing one's life.

In Discipleship 102 (Luke 9:57-10:24), our Lord was headed toward Jerusalem when he was confronted by three men who had their own hidden agendas when it came to the subject of discipleship. Jesus warned the first man who approached him that if he followed Him he would never have a home. The second man wanted to follow Jesus, but only after he first buried his father. A third man also wanted to follow Jesus, but he first wanted to go home and say goodbye to his family. It was at this point that Jesus disqualified all three because of their hidden agendas. He said to them, and to all who desire to follow him: "No one, after putting his hand to the plow and looking back, is fit for the kingdom of God" (Luke 9:62).

Now, let's consider a third element of discipleship from Luke 14:25-35. The scene has changed and we find our Lord facing a new crowd who wanted to follow him in Peraea. (Peraea is the land east of the Jordan river with the Sea of Galilee in the north and the Dead Sea in the south.) They had been anticipating the physical and spiritual blessings that would come to them because of their relationship with the Messiah, but since Israel's spiritual leaders had rejected their Messiah, the physical blessings were postponed. As tension continued to build up around him, Jesus needed more disciples to carry out his mission after his death and resurrection in Jerusalem. He did not want his disciples to follow him based on an emotional reaction to an exciting message, rather he sought people who would give up all that they held dear, even their own lives, to follow him.

As we continue, we will see that Jesus is building on this concept of discipleship by asking the question: "Have you calculated the cost of becoming my disciple?" If so, then…

We must be willing to hate our family

Luke 14:25-26

Now large crowds were going along with Him; and He turned and said to them, "If anyone comes to Me, and does not hate his own father and mother and wife and children and brothers and sisters…he cannot be My disciple."

Our Lord Jesus had reminded his disciples on more than one occasion of the purpose of his ministry on earth, saying: "I have not come to call righteous but sinners to repentance" (Luke: 5:32), and that "…the Son of Man has come to seek and to save that which was lost" (Luke 19:10). At this point in our Lord's life, we find him just a few months away from the cross of Calvary, preaching about the kingdom of God. As a result of his preaching, many men and women wanted to join him and the other disciples in their ministry. It was at this time that he needed to challenge them about the true cost of discipleship. In the days ahead anyone who was willing to follow him would have to join with him as he faced the full wrath of the Jewish leadership, as well as the political powers of the Roman Empire. For some this could mean arrest, jail, whippings, and death.

"If anyone comes after Me…." Within this idea of discipleship we find the same principles as we do in a marriage relationship—the leaving of family, the cleaving to a wife, and becoming one in body, soul and spirit. Before we commit ourselves to invite Jesus to be our Lord, we must first give this commitment the same serious consideration we would give to a marriage proposal because within that agreement we find the terms of servanthood and a willingness to die to self. David Gooding wrote: *Thousands have been and still are confronted with this choice right at the outset of their Christian lives. They see, as clearly as Saul of Tarsus saw, that salvation is a free gift. Equally clearly they see that confession of faith in Christ will cost them career, friends, family, perhaps life itself; and they have to decide between Christ and salvation on the one side and all else on the other side.* [1]

Jesus goes on to say, "…and [if he] does not hate his own…" This concept is best understood when we view it side by side with what our Lord said in Matthew 10:37:

[1] David Gooding, *According to Luke: A New Exposition of the Third Gospel,* © 1987, Eerdmans Publishing Co.; ISBN 0-8028-0316-4, paperback, 362 pages; Currently out of print.

"He who loves father or mother more than Me is not worthy of Me; and he who loves son or daughter more than Me is not worthy of Me."

In the context of Luke 14:26, our Lord was challenging those in the crowd who were thinking of following him that they would have to "hate" (or love less) their family members. The call to give one's loyalty to Jesus will at times be perceived particularly by unbelieving family members or friends as offensive, even hateful. Still, Jesus must be the final authority in everything a Christian does in life.

I was reminded of this principle of "loving less" the other day when I had an opportunity to think through the early days of our marriage. When Anne Marie committed to marry me, she was still living at home in Rabat, Morocco. She was surrounded by the security of her family, friends, religion and school. She enjoyed the sights, sounds and smells of a delightful French and Moroccan culture. We met in Rabat. There we grew in love, committed to marriage, exchanged vows, and moved into our first home where we lived for about a year. But we both knew that in time we would have to pack up and move to my home in Pennsylvania. When that day came, Anne Marie was asked to leave her family, friends and church, the sights, sounds and smells of that delightful French and Moroccan culture and, in essence, to "love less" all that she had held dear all of her life in order to be with me and together follow where our Lord was leading us.

That same thing must happen when we come to Christ. Have we calculated the cost of becoming his disciple? We must realize that to love Jesus Christ and to follow him means we must love our families less. But, there is another thing we must do. We must also come to the realization that…

We must be willing to hate our own life

Luke 14:26

If anyone comes to Me, and does not hate his own father and mother and wife and children and brothers and sisters, yes, and even his own life, he cannot be My disciple.

Our Lord had already challenged the twelve disciples in Luke 9:23 when he said, "If anyone wishes to come after Me, he must deny himself, and take up his cross daily and follow Me." To deny oneself means to choose by the power of the indwelling Holy Spirit to live daily in the spiritual reality that Paul shared with the Corinthians: "You are not your own; you have been bought with a price" (1 Corinthians 6:19-20). Or as C.E.B. Canfield put it:

To deny one's self...is to turn away from the idolatry of self-centeredness. Once we place our faith in Jesus as Lord and Savior we become his bondservants and we learn to live our lives to fulfill his will, not our own. We will need to learn to deny our self-confidence, our self-adequacy and our self-sufficiency which we were taught by the spirit of this age. Either Jesus is Lord of our lives or we are. We cannot have it both ways. And this is a process of learning which never ceases until we join him in eternity.

The key attitude of our new lives in Christ is to live out the words of our Lord, as prayed on the night before he willingly died on the cross of Calvary for our sins, "[Father], if You are willing, remove this cup from Me; *yet not My will, but Yours be done*" (Luke 22:42, emphasis mine). Of the original twelve disciples, ten were willing to hate their own lives and died un-timely deaths as martyrs. Only John was imprisoned by the Romans for his faith in Christ and later was released to die a natural death in Asia. Judas loved his life more than Christ and in the end, committed suicide.

When we give up our rights, however, others receive life. There was a wonderful segment on ABC television news once about a woman who did just this. She had twelve children of her own and she took in the homeless, the sick and the hungry, and bathed and fed them. "This helps restore the sense of dignity of those less fortunate," she said. She was denying herself that others might live. This is a critical part of Christian discipleship.

In 1979, Chet Bitterman arrived in Bogota, Colombia to begin work among the Carijona Indians. Before his arrival, Chet wrote in his diary: "Maybe this is just some kind of self-inflated martyr complex, but I find this recurring thought that perhaps God will call me to be martyred for him in his service in Colombia. I am willing." Two years later, Chet was captured by terrorists who demanded that his mission, Wycliffe Translators, leave Colombia immediately. Wycliffe understandably refused their demands. Seven weeks later, Chet's body was discovered in an abandoned bus. He had loved his life less than his Lord and had paid the ultimate price.

Have we calculated the cost of becoming a disciple of Christ? Not only must we come to the realization that to love Jesus Christ and follow him we must be willing to "hate" (or love less) our families and our own life, but also...

We must be willing to carry our cross

Luke 14:27-32

"Whoever does not carry his own cross and come after Me cannot be My disciple. For which one of you, when he wants to build a tower, does not first sit down and calculate the cost to see if he has enough to complete it? Otherwise, when he has laid a foundation and is not able to finish, all who observe it begin to ridicule him, saying, 'This man began to build and was not able to finish.' Or what king, when he sets out to meet another king in battle, will not first sit down and consider whether he is strong enough with ten thousand men to encounter the one coming against him with twenty thousand? Or else, while the other is still far away, he sends a delegation and asks for terms of peace."

In Luke 9:23 the Lord told his disciples: "If anyone wishes to come after Me, he must deny himself, and take up his cross daily and follow Me." Months later, the Lord drove another nail of truth into the hearts of those around him who expressed a desire to follow him. Wanting them to get a full picture of what they were asking, he declared: "Whoever does not carry his own cross and come after Me cannot be my disciple" (Luke 14:27).

The cross, which was an instrument of shame, humiliation and death, was used by the Roman authorities to punish criminals. When the Jews watched a criminal pick up a cross and follow a squad of Roman soldiers to the hill of Calvary, they all knew he was going to his death. Of course, the criminal took up his cross under duress, but Christians must do this willingly by the power of the indwelling Holy Spirit. Now, to "carry our cross" does not mean simply tolerating our mother-in-law, or a handicap or sickness. Rather, to carry our cross first means that we are willing to admit that it was because of our sins of envy, rebellion, pride, lust, murder, adultery, slander, etc. that Jesus died on the cross on our behalf. When we placed our faith in him and in his death, we too died once and for all to the power of sin. And now, because he lives, we are able to live a new, resurrected life of righteousness by his resurrection power (c.f. Romans 6).

Secondly, to carry our cross means we have a daily reminder that our flesh needs to be put to death. The apostle Paul wrote to the Galatians: "Now those who belong to Christ Jesus have crucified the flesh with its passions and desires. If we live by the Spirit, let us also walk by the Spirit" (Galatians 5:24-25). We are not to coddle or cuddle our flesh, nor are we to tolerate it or give it any encouragement. Rather, we are to reject it, together with its selfish desires. We must nail the "flesh" to the cross daily by the power of the indwelling Holy Spirit.

And thirdly, to carry our cross, according to Paul, means that if Jesus is Lord, then "...we who live are constantly being delivered over to death for Jesus' sake, so that the life of Jesus also may be manifested in our mortal flesh. So death works in us, but life in you" (2 Corinthians 4:11-12). In his book, *The Cross Of Christ*, John R. W. Stott writes: *The cross undermines our self-righteousness. We stand before it only with a bowed head and a broken spirit...and there we remain until the Lord Jesus speaks to our hearts his word of pardon and acceptance, and we, gripped by his love and brimful of thanksgiving, go out into the world to live our lives in his service.*[2]

To go out into the world actually means to enter into the world of the "breathing dead." I can hardly count the number of times in the past few days that I have heard sports figures who are involved in youth programs say on television that what they teach young people is how to be the best, how to try harder and not quit, etc. But none of this really works, does it? It's all of the flesh, and as Paul says, "the flesh profits nothing" (c.f. 2 Timothy 4:8).

So, again, we must take up our cross daily and as Jesus says, "follow [Him]...." Many Jewish people were willing to follow Jesus for awhile, but then they left him because he continued to offer them a spiritual kingdom while what they really wanted was a political kingdom. However, a true disciple would not only deny himself and take up his cross, but would also follow him wherever he led. Sometimes this would involve even physical death on a cross. And as I mentioned earlier, several of the original twelve would suffer death in this way. To follow Jesus means to walk in obedience to his word so that our lives bring glory to him and joy to our hearts. We must follow him each and every day with the view to crucifying the flesh, and if necessary, even to give up our physical life for his name's sake.

Most of you are aware of the hazards of living in Colombia, South America. I remember a trip I made to that country in the late 1980's with Ed Woodhall and Carl Gallivan. We had heard stories of how the drug barons had systematically murdered 54 judges and forced another 108 officials to leave their posts. Not only were the lives of those ministers of justice put on the line, but the lives of the ministers of the gospel of Jesus Christ were also threatened. Miquel Mosquera, a pastor and attorney who, at that time, was serving the Lord in Medellin, the capital city, was quoted as saying: *For me to live is Christ, to die is gain. Christ is the reason for my living, and if my death contributes toward the salvation of the people of Medellin, then I am willing to take the chance. Christ accepted the risk of living in the midst of a lost and corrupt world, a world that took him to the cross. Why should I not risk myself?* In other words, if his death would contribute toward the salvation of the people of Medellin, Miquel was willing to suffer death.

On another occasion a number of years ago, a young Colombian woman took our team on a tour of the slums of Medellin so we could see her ministry there. She worked among the desperately poor, mainly ex-convicts who were not permitted to work and earn a living for themselves. We saw such dangerous places that we feared for her life every minute but she, too, was willing to die so that her flock should live. That is what it means to be a follower of Jesus Christ.

Jesus' own disciple Peter once boasted that he would follow him anywhere, even unto death (c.f. Matthew 26:34; Mark 14:30; Luke 22:61). But Jesus, knowing better, responded to that declaration, in effect saying, "Oh, really? Today Satan wants to sift you like wheat. After you return from denying me, strengthen your brothers (Luke 22:31-32). Peter, unless the Spirit of God lives in you and empowers you, you can't talk like that. If you are going to follow me, you will suffer, but you will have much joy, too, as my disciple."

After laying down the terms for being a disciple, Jesus goes on to illustrate just how he counted the cost before he came into the world to save us from our sins. First, he tells a story about a tower (Luke 14:28-29): "For which one of you, when he wants to build a tower, does not first sit down and calculate the cost to see if he has enough to complete it? Otherwise, when he has laid a foundation and is not able to finish, all who observe it begin to ridicule him, saying, 'This man began to build and was not able to finish.'"

As he surveys the crowd, the Lord reminds them of a basic principle of life: If a man needs to build a tower in a field in order to keep watch over his fields or flocks, isn't it only natural for him to first "calculate the cost" before he begins to build it? Otherwise, if he merely has a vision to build a tower, and in the heat of the moment runs out and purchases some material, to discover later that he has only enough to build a foundation and cannot finish the project, onlookers would see that he did not take the time to fully "calculate the cost" of his tower. As they pass by each day, they ridicule him, saying, "This man began to build and was not able to finish."

Jesus' came to earth to build a tower, or more specifically, the "Spiritual Kingdom of God," the "Body of Christ," "the church." In Caesarea Philippi, after Peter had declared him the "Christ of God," Jesus said to Peter "...and upon that rock I will build My church and the gates of Hades shall not overpower it" (Matthew 16:17-18). And yet, before Jesus came to earth, he sat down with his Father and together they "calculated the cost" of this tower. The cost

[2] R.W. Stott, *The Cross of Christ* (see page 4).

would be the life of the innocent Lamb of God, crucified on the cross of Calvary for the sins of humanity against God the Father.

The Lord did not come to earth with some half-baked plan for the salvation of man and fail. No! He came with a complete plan, one with a beginning, middle, and culminating in his death for our life. As Paul wrote, "[The Son of God] emptied Himself, taking the form of a bond-servant, and being made in the likeness of man. Being found in appearance as a man, He humbled Himself by becoming obedient to the point of death, even death on a cross" (Philippians 2:7-8). Because of his resurrection and ascension, all who are willing to become his disciples have been given the Holy Spirit who enables each to make disciples in their generation until our Lord returns.

Jesus tells a second story about the cost of a battle (14:31-32): "Or what king, when he sets out to meet another king in battle, will not first sit down and consider whether he is strong enough with ten thousand men to encounter the one coming against him with twenty thousand? Or else, while the other is still far away, he sends a delegation and asks for terms of peace." Here our Lord uses another familiar, and yet basic principle concerning war: No king under attack would begin a war with his enemy without first sitting down with his generals and "taking counsel" to see whether or not he was strong enough to defeat him. The fact that he had only 10,000 men while his enemy had 20,000 is not the issue, but whether his army of 10,000 is strong enough to defeat the 20,000 men. If not, then he would be wise to send a delegation and ask for terms for peace.

Our Lord came to build his church, saying that the "gates of Hades shall not overpower it" (Matthew 16:18). Jesus was in a battle against a spiritual foe who was determined to destroy the church he was building. He wanted faithful men and women to join him in the building, as well as the battle. In the case of our Lord, we know that he and his Father sat down and took counsel against Satan and his army in the heavenlies. It would be a spiritual battle against Satan for the souls of men, women and children, and the issue was: Was he strong enough to defeat this arch enemy?

After taking counsel with the Father, he decided to enter the battle and to defeat the enemy by his voluntary death on the cross and resurrection from the dead. This King was willing to give up all he had so that others might live. Through his death and resurrection he defeated Satan, and God was then able to "deliver us from the domain of darkness, and transfer us to the kingdom of His well-beloved Son, in whom we have redemption, the forgiveness of sins" (Colossians 1:13-14). At the same time, "...God highly exalted Him and bestowed on Him the name which is above every name, that at the name of Jesus every knee should bow, of those who are in heaven, and on earth, and under the earth, and that every tongue should confess that Jesus Christ is Lord to the glory of God the Father" (Philippians 2: 9-11).

Jesus was willing to count the cost to build the church and win the battle. In light of these spiritual realities we can see that the call to discipleship is a serious step. 1) We must love our family less then we love the Lord; 2) We must be willing to love our own life less; and, 3) We must be willing to take up our cross and follow him wherever he leads us. Finally...

We must be willing to give up our "stuff"

Luke 14:33-35

"So then, none of you can be My disciple who does not give up all his own possessions. Therefore, salt is good; but if even salt has become tasteless, with what will it be seasoned? It is useless either for the soil or for the manure pile; it is thrown out. He who has ears to hear, let him hear."

Our Lord challenges these "would-be disciples" to seriously "calculate the cost" before they set out to follow him. They must be willing to give up all of their earthly possessions in the sense that they give them over to his control. We no longer "own" anything of material worth. Rather, we understand that we are stewards of God's possessions. At times our Lord may ask some of his true disciples to literally give up their earthly possessions to serve him in a certain manner, and he expects them to do so gladly. The important thing is that whosoever desires to follow him must be inwardly free from worldly-mindedness, covetousness and selfishness, and be wholly devoted to him.

It is of interest to note that Judas would have been in this audience listening for the third time to this kind of sermon. As the treasurer for the disciples, he was quietly stealing money from the purse in order to purchase a field. The things of this earth were very important to him, as well as to many others in the crowd.

Or take the struggle the rich young ruler had after he had asked Jesus, "What shall I do to obtain eternal life?" Jesus admitted that the young man had kept the commands, but he lacked one thing, so he said, "...sell all that you possess, and distribute it to the poor, and you shall have treasure in heaven, and come and follow Me...When he had heard these things, he became very sad, for he was extremely rich" (Luke 18:18-27). The Lord wanted the man, not his money. In this case, the rich young ruler was held prisoner by his wealth and was not free to follow Jesus. The issue, of course, is who or what you are serving? Jesus said in the Sermon on the Mount, "No one can serve two masters; for either he will hate the one and love the other or he will hold to one and despise the other. You cannot serve God and riches" (Matthew 5:24).

Now, just what did Jesus mean concerning the "salt"? Salt was used both to arrest corruption and to add flavor to food. When it was good salt it was of great value. Our Lord, in his Sermon on the Mount, had told his disciples, "You are the salt of the earth; but if the salt has become tasteless, how will it be made salty again? It is good for nothing any more, except to be thrown out and trampled under foot by men" (Matthew 5:13). He had walked among the religious leaders long enough to see that many of them who once had a love for the Lord and his Word were now bound up in self-interest and legalism. When the salt of their lives was poured out on the Jewish community to arrest corruption and add spiritual flavor, they were found wanting; they had lost their value and their lives had become useless and tasteless. At the same time, Jesus was looking for men and women who would follow him even into the fires of persecution and death, if necessary, without losing their spiritual flavor.

Once at PBC, someone came to me and said there was a man sitting at the back who appeared to be destitute and perhaps needed help. When I saw him, I said, "You've been here before, haven't you?" "Yes," he replied. He was a nice-looking man. He said he was in need of food and money—just twenty dollars. Now we have protocol at PBC that we typically follow concerning these matters. But this time, the Lord said to me, "Leave it alone. Just deal with it. The man needs food and money? Just give it to him." So I gave him what he needed. Then he told me he had a friend in his truck that also needed food, so I got food for him too.

Something moved me and I said to him, "Can I pray for you." He said, "Yes." I put my arm around him and I said, "Lord, please give this man back his dignity, his image, his significance. Give him back a reason for living, a reason for life as you designed it to be lived. And give him back a view of who you really are in your Son Jesus. Give him life; in Jesus' name, Amen." I stepped back and said, "I wish you well today." He looked at me, and then he hugged me. "Thank you," he said. He got into his truck and drove away. It's not so hard, is it? It's just salt; one more day in this man's life—salt, life, flavor, arresting corruption. God provided that. I was busy being religious, and then God said, "That's enough religion. Come over here. I want you to get practical."

Norval Geldenhuys wrote: *A great deal is entailed in being a disciple of Jesus. But the enrichment of one's whole* *life and the eternal welfare resulting from it is still much greater and more glorious. In addition, we must remember: not to be a disciple of Jesus means to be a disciple of the powers of darkness. And to be a servant of the world and of sin costs incalculably more then to be a disciple of Jesus—the price of it is the loss of the highest happiness in this life and darkness and affliction of soul throughout eternity. How insignificant is the price of self-renunciation in His service in comparison with the price to be paid for rejecting Him!*[3]

When Jesus said: "He who has an ear to hear let him hear" he was saying, in effect: "Listen carefully to my words for your whole life; now and into eternity because both depend on it." Remember, Peter and Judas both listened to those very words.

Have you and I calculated the cost of becoming a disciple of Christ? Here, again, are the requirements of Discipleship 103:

1. We must be willing to hate our family or we cannot be his disciple.

2. We must be willing to hate our own life or we cannot be his disciple.

3. We must be willing to carry our own cross or we cannot be his disciple.

4. We must be willing to give up our material possessions or we cannot be his disciple.

There are no other options. We can neither audit the course, nor should we expect to fail because we have been given his Spirit.

I want to conclude by sharing with you more of Dudley's story about his walk with the young man on the beach.

[Dudley] said, "It means you want to be a follower of Jesus Christ and truly His disciple?" He affirmed, "Yes." I asked him to tell me how he heard about Jesus and why he asked him to be the Lord and Savior of his life. He explained to me in detail what happened. I told him, "Jesus said that 'if anyone wishes to come after Me, let him deny himself, and take up his cross and follow Me.'" I explained that to be a disciple of Jesus we must be willing to lay aside our desires and our goals and our expectations for our life and he will give us new ones...ones that come

---

[3] Norval Geldenhuys, *Commentary on the Gospel of Luke*, (Copyright and publisher unknown). ASIN: B00005VNCY

from the heart…ones that will produce life…eternal life….in us and in the lives of others.

I again asked, "Are you ready to do this? Are you ready to pay this price? Are you ready for the adventures that lie ahead?" and he said, "Yes." And I said, "Then come with me. It's time for you to make a public declaration of your faith."

As we walked down into the water, he turned and faced a beach full of curious onlookers. Then he looked at me and made a verbal declaration of his faith in Jesus Christ as his Lord and Savior. It was then that I had the privilege of baptizing my son Joshua in the gentle waves of the bay of St. Jean de Luz.

Joshua was nine years old at the time. I ask you, and I say to myself as well, is there any reason why you would want to live any other way? I hope not. What a waste of your life—to live any other way than as a disciple of Jesus Christ. I beg of you: Don't choose the other way. Being his disciple brings life, but if you're not a disciple of his, then you are a disciple of the powers of darkness. There's no other option. The choice is yours.

A Disciple of Jesus...

By Dallas Willard

As a disciple of Jesus, I am with him by choice and by grace, learning from him how to live in the Kingdom of God...

His life flowing through mine...

I am learning from Jesus to live my life as he would live my life if he were I.

I am not necessarily learning to do everything he did, but I am learning how to do everything I do in the manner that he did all that he did.[1]

ℬ　　℺

The New Testament is a book about disciples, by disciples, and for disciples of Jesus Christ... Who among Christians today is a disciple of Jesus in any substantive sense of the word disciple? A disciple is a learner, a student, an apprentice - a practitioner, even if only a beginner. The New Testament literature, which must be allowed to define our terms if we are ever to get our bearing in the Way with Christ, makes this clear. In that context, disciples of Jesus are people who do not just profess certain views as their own but apply their growing understanding of life in the Kingdom of Heaven to every aspect of their life on earth.[2]

[1]Excerpts are taken from *The Divine Conspiracy: Rediscovering Our Hidden Life in God.* © 1998 by Dallas Willard. HarperCollins Publishers, New York, NY. P. 283

[2]*The Great Omission,* © 2006 HarperCollins Publishers, San Francisco, CA. Pp. 4, 11.

DISCIPLESHIP: A HIGH CALLING!

Discipleship 104

Luke 17:1-19

In October 1955, I entered a cold, empty tomb in Jerusalem, the very tomb according to many, where the body of Christ was placed following his death. I was a spiritually bankrupt man. I had no resources left, having burned them all, and I had finally come to the realization that I needed to change my life, radically. There, in that tomb, I gave my life to the resurrected Christ and that very day my new life in Christ began. I didn't realize at the time that I was embarking on such a high calling—becoming a disciple of Jesus Christ.

In the intervening years, I have since learned that this high calling is actually a "process." When Jesus said to his first disciples, "Follow me and I will make you to become fishers of men," and they immediately dropped their fishing nets and followed him, it was just the beginning of the process for them. I'm grateful that this *is* a process, and that God is patient and loving toward his disciples as he leads them into spiritual maturity.

As we have been learning in our studies in the gospel of Luke, the Lord's mission on earth was to "...seek and to save that which was lost" (Luke 19:10). Once we place our faith in him as our Lord and Savior, his desire for us is that we join him as disciples in his mission on this earth—the redemption of men, women and children from the kingdom of darkness. I have likened this process to a "curriculum" for discipleship. In Discipleship 101 we learned that as disciples of Jesus Christ we must deny ourselves and take up our cross daily and follow him (c.f. Luke 9:18-27).

In Discipleship 102 Jesus warned that we are not to try to follow him with our own agenda. Rather, when he calls us we must be willing to leave our security, family and friends immediately. For, as he said, "No one after putting his hand to the plow and looking back, is fit for the kingdom of God" (Luke 9:57-10:24).

In Discipleship 103 Jesus said that all who desire to follow him and become his disciples must be willing to hate (or to love *less*) their families and even their own lives and give up all their possessions. (Luke 14:25-35)

To help us see how some of these truths are worked out in flesh and blood, the following is an unknown author's impression of the life of the apostle Paul once he came into a vital relationship with Jesus on the Damascus Road: *He is a man without the care of making friends, without the hope or desire of worldly goods, without the appre-hension of worldly loss, without the care of life and without the fear of death...A man of one thought—the Gospel of Christ; a man of one purpose—the glory of God. A fool and content to be reckoned a fool for Christ...He must speak or he must die, and though he should die, he will speak. He has no rest but hastens over land and sea, over rocks and trackless deserts. He cries aloud and spares not, and will not be hindered. In prisons he lifts up his voice and in the tempests of the ocean he is not silent. Before awful councils and kings, he witnesses in behalf of the truth. Nothing can quench his voice but death, and even in the article of death, before the knife has severed his head from his body, he speaks, he prays, he testifies, he confesses, he beseeches, he wars, and at length he blesses the cruel people.*[1]

As we continue in our study on discipleship, we will see that as our Lord moves closer to the cross, the high calling of discipleship continues to be his focus. Therefore, in Discipleship l04 (Luke 17:1-19) our Lord reminds his disciples of this high calling by encouraging them: 1) Not to become stumbling blocks to sinners who are seeking him; 2) To be willing to rebuke and to forgive sinners who repent of their sins; 3) To grow in their faith towards him; and, 4) To serve him with a thankful heart.

Beware of becoming a stumbling block

Luke 17:1-2

He said to His disciples, "It is inevitable that stumbling blocks come, but woe to him through whom they come! It would be better for him if a millstone were hung around his neck and he were thrown into the sea, than that he would cause one of these little ones to stumble."

Jesus had been teaching the gospel to the tax-gatherers and sinners who had assembled around him (Luke 15:1). But the Pharisees were grumbling, "This man receives sinners and eats with them." They were inferring that Jesus could not possibly be the Son of God because to eat with sinners was tantamount to agreeing with their immoral

---

[1]William MacDonald, *True Discipleship*, © 1975,Walterick Publishing; ISBN 0937396508.

lifestyle. They thought it wrong that these sinners, who had probably broken all ten of the commandments as well as the traditions of Judaism, should be offered forgiveness. In fact, the Pharisees regarded this as too simple a solution in light of the fact that most of them had spent their entire lives seeking to live up to the requirements of the Law and its traditions. Our Lord sought to show them the secrets of the kingdom of God through parables and stories, but up until now none of them had accepted his gracious invitation of salvation.

As Jesus listened to the grumblings of the Pharisees while in the presence of the sinners who where seeking to understand spiritual truth, he used this as a "teachable moment." He wanted them to love the Pharisees but not to follow in their footsteps when it came to tempting others to sin. "It is inevitable that stumbling blocks should come…" said Jesus.

The original meaning of the phrase translated "stumbling block" is to tempt someone to sin. It is always used metaphorically in the New Testament, and ordinarily of anything that arouses prejudice or becomes a hindrance to others or causes them to fall by the way. In this context, our Lord is warning his disciples that as sinners are drawn to the gospel of the kingdom it was inevitable that some would trip over a stumbling block placed in their path by someone opposed to the messenger, as well as to the message of salvation. That is the reality of opposition in a fallen world. Within a few months Jesus and his cross would become an offense to the Jewish leadership (1 Corinthians 23), and it has remained so in every generation to this very day.

"…But woe to him through whom they come!" said Jesus. "It would be better for him if a millstone were hung around his neck and he were thrown into the sea, than that he should cause one of these little ones to stumble." In that culture everyone knew of the various types of millstones that were used to crush grain. Smaller millstones were for home use, but when it came to harvest time farmers used much larger millstones, up to four or five feet in diameter. The grain was placed on a base stone and then the millstone (which had a hole in the middle as big as a man's head) was lifted up to the stationary stone which had a center peg as an axle. Once the millstone was in place it could be turned around in a circle by a mule or camel until the grain was crushed into fine flour.

As Jesus was saying this you can be sure he was warning his disciples about their future ministry, but at the same time he was looking at the lifestyle of the Pharisees. They were the very stumbling blocks that he had in mind as he observed them trying to confuse and discourage the open-hearted tax-gatherers and sinners. The warning is very serious.

David Gooding wrote: …*No sin against a fellowman can possibly be more serious than to do something by act or word to stumble him in his faith, or to break that faith, in God, in the deity of Christ, in the authority of His Word, in the value of his redemption or the reality of his salvation. Therefore, if anyone caused "these little ones" to stumble on their way to Jesus, the consequences for the people responsible for that occurrence will be so grave when they come into the presence of God it would be better for that person to take his own life rather than to go on living and turning others away from Jesus.*[2] John encouraged the Ephesian church saying, "The one who loves his brother abides in the Light and there is no cause for stumbling in him" (1 John 2:10). They don't stumble and they don't cause others to stumble because they are living by the power of the Holy Spirit and walking in the light of the truth of Jesus Christ.

Several years ago a team of men from PBC were invited to go to a Christian college in another state to minister during their "Spiritual Emphasis" week. We were invited to speak in chapel, at dormitory meetings in the evenings, to teach Bible classes in the homes of the professors, attend classes with the students, etc. It was a challenging and enjoyable week. However, in the course of the week it became evident that several professors were forsaking the principle of intellectual honesty in their Bible courses and deliberately seeking to undermine the faith of their young students.

At the end of the week, our team was invited to speak to the whole faculty. I wasn't sure what I was going to say since I didn't know which teachers were responsible for placing stumbling blocks in the path of "these little ones." My heart was pounding as I asked the Lord to give me the words to say so that people would not miss the point. Several members of our team addressed the college President and his staff, and then I was asked to say a few words. I must say that I can't take any credit for what I said because the way I spoke was foreign, even to me. Following a few words of thanks for some of the good things that had occurred during the week, I said, "I have become acutely aware from a number of conversations I have had with students on this campus that with full knowledge several teachers in this Christian college are placing stumbling blocks in the spiritual paths of these young students. Jesus has warned that if you are doing that, it would be better that someone put a millstone around your neck and throw you into the sea" (or, in other words, *that you contemplate suicide*). The President thanked me and the meeting was over. Several teachers thanked me but I couldn't help notice the many who left in a hurry. We were not invited back.

[2] David Gooding, *According to Luke…* (see page 12).

Discipleship is a high calling. We must beware of becoming a stumbling block and we must…

Be willing to rebuke and forgive

Luke 17:3-4

"Be on your guard! If your brother sins, rebuke him; and if he repents, forgive him. And if he sins against you seven times a day, and returns to you seven times, saying, 'I repent,' forgive him."

Here Jesus goes on to give three commands that we are to carry out within the Christian community as true disciples who have been forgiven all of our sins.

Command #1: Be on your guard! Speaking of tempting others to sin, look to your own life first and make sure that you are not becoming a stumbling block to those seeking to come into the kingdom. This command has the same idea as our Lord's words in Matthew 7:4-5: "…how can you say to your brother, 'Let me take the speck out of your eye,' and behold, the log is in your own eye? You hypocrite, first take the log out of your own eye; and then you will see clearly enough to take the speck out of your brother's eye."

Command #2: Rebuke a sinning brother. "If your brother sins, rebuke him…" If a disciple should see or find out about a brother who has sinned in the sight of God (as in the immediate context of placing a stumbling block in the way of a sinner who is seeking to come into the kingdom of God), he should rebuke him. That is, look for an opportunity where he is able to hear you and have an open heart to repent of his sin. The Lord had already spoken on this subject when he said to his disciples, as recorded in Matthew 18:15: "And if your brother sins, go and reprove him in private; if he listens to you, you have won your brother. But if he does not listen to you, take one or two more with you, so that by the mouth of two or three witnesses every fact may be confirmed. And if he refuses to listen to them, tell it to the church; and if he refuses to listen to even the church, let him be to you as a Gentile and a tax-gatherer [a non-believer whom we would seek, in love, to win into the kingdom]."

Command #3: Forgive him. "…And if he repents, forgive him." If your brother or sister is willing to listen to your loving rebuke and confess, turning away from the sinful activity toward God again, forgive them. This is not a suggestion; it is a command from Jesus.

The parable of the prodigal son is a wonderful example of a true, repentant heart; a heart that is ready to forgive. Speaking of the son, Luke wrote, "But when he came to his senses, he said… 'I will get up and go to my father, and will say to him, "Father, I have sinned against heaven, and in your sight; I am no longer worthy to be called your son; make me as one of your hired men."'" (Luke 15:17-19) Just as this father had already forgiven his sinful son in his heart, even before he confessed his sin, we too must fill our hearts with the spirit of forgiveness towards those who have wronged us or others.

Do you remember when the Lord had taught the disciples how to pray? He said: "And forgive us our debts, as we also have forgiven our debtors…For if you forgive others for their transgressions, your heavenly Father will also forgive you. But if you do not forgive others, then your Father will not forgive your transgressions" (Matthew 6:12, 14-15). And even before that, Peter had asked the Lord: "Lord, how often shall my brother sin against me and I forgive him? Up to seven times?" Jesus said to him, "I do not say to you, up to seven times, but up to seventy times seven" (Matthew 18:21-22). "And if he sins against you seven times a day and returns to you seven times, saying 'I repent,' forgive him" (Matthew 18:35). You see, it must be immediate, definite, incisive, and made in a spirit of genuine forgiveness.

Further, Paul wrote to the Ephesian church whose members were having difficulties with each other: "Do not grieve the Holy Spirit of God, by whom you were sealed for the day of redemption. Let all bitterness and wrath and anger and clamor and slander be put away from you, along with all malice. Be kind to one another, tender-hearted, forgiving each other, just as God in Christ also has forgiven you" (Ephesians 4:30-32).

So, why all this talk of forgiveness if one truly repents of his sins against you or me? It's because our Lord understands our frailty. We were born in Adam and sin has taken a fearsome toll in our lives. God knows that we are still in the process of learning about our new nature in the Second Adam, who is Christ himself, so we need to be patient.

Most people don't plan on being hurtful toward others any more than they plan on being angry, jealous, envious or malicious. Each morning I ask God to use me and make me to be a righteous man. When something goes wrong later in the day, when I'm angry at someone and that person is angry at me, I ask myself what happened. I didn't plan this; in fact, quite the opposite. Let us remember, first of all, that God *in Christ* has forgiven us. Secondly, we have never before been in this arena where we are known as children of God. And thirdly, God is *maturing* us so that we will be like Jesus—the process is not yet finished. We need to remember the wise and godly individual who said, "Be patient with me, God is not finished with me yet!"

Speaking of how the "old Adam" expresses itself when Jesus is not allowed to be Lord, I read last week the end of the long and tragic story of Marine Col. William R. Higgins. This man was serving with the United Nations peacekeeping force in Lebanon when he was seized by rebel forces on February 17, 1988. According to a videotape, he was killed on July 31, 1989. His body was recently found and returned to the United States for burial. After the burial services, Higgins' widow, Marine Corps Major Robin Higgins, issued a statement urging Americans not to forgive the hostage takers. She said, "If we forgive, if we forget, if we thank these savages, then we are merely inviting them at a time and place they will select to kill again; shame on us if we do!"

This is not how a disciple of Jesus should respond. A true disciple understands that it's only the grace of God that can change an unforgiving, hard heart to a forgiving one. Only God can do this so that a heart is willing to forgive such a wrong. It's interesting that Terry Anderson, another hostage who was released recently, in response to the question, "Can you forgive your captives?" said, "Life is too short. I'm a Christian; we have been called to forgive."

To be a disciple of Christ is a high calling. We must beware of becoming a stumbling block, be willing to rebuke and forgive a repentant sinner, and be willing to…

Ask Jesus to increase our faith

Luke 17:5-10

The apostles said to the Lord, "Increase our faith!" And the Lord said, "If you had faith like a mustard seed, you would say to this mulberry tree, 'Be uprooted and be planted in the sea'; and it would obey you. Which of you, having a slave plowing or tending sheep, will say to him when he has come in from the field, 'Come immediately and sit down to eat'? But will he not say to him, 'Prepare something for me to eat, and properly clothe yourself and serve me while I eat and drink; and afterward you may eat and drink'? He does not thank the slave because he did the things which were commanded, does he? So you too, when you do all the things which are commanded you, say, 'We are unworthy slaves; we have done only that which we ought to have done.'"

In light of our Lord's commands, the disciples felt spiritually weak in their faith. Yet Jesus never asks any of his true followers to do anything apart from him. As they placed their small faith in him for each new situation, he would accomplish his will in and through them. Here Jesus uses the illustration of one of nature's smallest seeds, the mus-

tard seed. As small as this seed is it still has within it the principle of life: it is a living seed and it will grow. At that moment the disciples' faith was small, but Jesus encouraged them to start trusting him, and in time, in the midst of the most difficult tasks they were called to, their faith would grow to such a point that if they needed to cast a mulberry tree into the sea, it would be so. They had faith. What they really needed was to be reminded to focus on the Lord rather than on the immediate circumstances or demands.

As our Lord was preparing to go to the cross, he was also preparing the disciples to carry on the good news of the kingdom after his death, burial and resurrection. He was preparing them with the knowledge that they would become involved in a spiritual battle as they sought to redeem men and women from the kingdom of darkness and deliver them into the kingdom of light. Thus, he wanted them to become faithful disciples, men with the same hearts as those referred to in Luke 12:35-36: "Be dressed in readiness, and keep your lamps lit. Be like men who are waiting for their master when he returns from the wedding feast, so that they may immediately open the door to him when he comes…"

While we are on this earth, we are called to be faithful disciples in the midst of the spiritual battle for the souls of men and women. Our Lord has already commanded his disciples: 1) To not place stumbling blocks in the way of men and women who want to come into the kingdom of God; 2) To prepare their hearts to rebuke a brother, as well as forgive one who repents; and, 3) To grow in their faith in him so they could be greatly used in his plan of evangelism in the age of the Spirit and the building of his church.

Disciples should not come to the house after a long day in the field hoping that the master will ask them to sit and eat with him, even before they prepare his meal, or expect him stop in the midst of the battle to thank them for their faithfulness. It's time for us to take our responsibility for discipleship very seriously. We are called to be disciples *by the grace of God.* You and I who were once his enemies are now his disciples. Rejoice, remain faithful, and be thankful. And at the end of the battle, Luke says, "Blessed are those slaves whom the master will find on the alert when he comes; truly I say to you, that he will gird himself to serve, and have them recline at the table, and will come up and wait on them" (12:37).

I remember hearing the story of a faithful missionary couple who came back to this country following many difficult years of ministry in Africa. As their ship docked in New York harbor they heard a band on the dock playing welcome music for a returning passenger. There were hundreds of people gathered, waiting to greet their loved one. The missionary couple hoped to have someone from their mission board greet them, but by the time they came down the gangplank the band and the welcoming crowds had all gone their separate ways. All that was left to greet them were a few seagulls and the trash from the celebration that had been held earlier on the dock.

Not knowing what to do next, they walked a few blocks, carrying their suitcases in silence. Finally, they found a run-down hotel and checked in for the evening. As they sat in the dimly lit room, the husband could not contain himself any longer. In anger and frustration he cried out, "Honey, we worked so hard all these years. We have been faithful to our Lord, to our calling, to our mission board and to our people in Africa. You would have thought that someone from our board would have met us and welcomed us home, wouldn't you?" After a moment of silence, his wife reminded him of their eternal hope: "But honey, we aren't home yet!" she said.

Being a disciple of Christ is a high calling. We must beware of becoming a stumbling block, be willing to rebuke and to forgive a repentant sinner, and continue to ask the Lord to increase our small but living faith in him so that we may serve him from a heart of love and faithfulness. Also, as disciples of Jesus Christ…

We are called to be thankful servants

Luke 17:11-19

While He was on the way to Jerusalem, He was passing between Samaria and Galilee. As He entered a village, ten leprous men who stood at a distance met Him; and they raised their voices, saying, "Jesus, Master, have mercy on us!" When He saw them, He said to them, "Go and show yourselves to the priests." And as they were going, they were cleansed.

Now one of them, when he saw that he had been healed, turned back, glorifying God with a loud voice, and he fell on his face at His feet, giving thanks to Him. And he was a Samaritan. Then Jesus answered and said, "Were there not ten cleansed? But the nine—where are they? "Was no one found who returned to give glory to God, except this foreigner?" And He said to him, "Stand up and go; your faith has made you well."

This parable reminded Luke of an incident that occurred a little earlier as Jesus and his disciples were traveling south toward Jerusalem on the border between Samaria and Galilee before they crossed over the Jordan River into Peraea (modern Jordan). Ten leprous men came out to meet Jesus.

It must have been a terrible sight to see so many men banded together, their flesh rotting away from their bodies. The smell would have driven away anyone who came across their path. But not Jesus; he had come to save the lost.

These men stood at a distance and, having heard of Jesus from people in Galilee and Samaria, called out like a choir in unison, "Jesus, Master, have pity on us!" He responded just as he has many times before, only this time rather than touching them, he asked them to place their faith in him and go to the temple in Jerusalem, saying: "Go and show yourselves to the priests." According to chapters 13 and 14 of Leviticus, if a leper was cured he was to go to the priest to demonstrate God's grace, and then the priest would publicly restore that man or woman back into fellowship within the community. In this case, as all ten placed they faith in Jesus' command and began to walk south towards Jerusalem, completely healed.

In recording this parable, Luke notes that one of the leprous men was different from the other nine. Once this man realized he was completely healed at the word of Jesus, he did three things. First, he turned back towards Jesus. Secondly, he began praising God. Finally, he fell on his face at the feet of Jesus, thanking him. Then Luke drops a bombshell: this man was a Samaritan! Remember, the Samaritan people had intermarried with Gentiles, set up their own religion in Samaria instead of Jerusalem, studied only the first five books of Moses, and built their own temple and worshipped God in Samaria. They were hated by the Jews. But now, this healed Samaritan was thanking a Jew and bowing at his feet.

Jesus asked three questions of this man and then blessed him: "Were there not ten cleansed?" "But the nine, where are they?" "Were none found who turned back to give glory to God, except this foreigner?" And he said to the man, "Rise, and go your way; your faith has made you well ("well" being same word in Greek as the word for "salvation").

Notably, Jesus was grieved over the lack of thankfulness and praise that was due to the God of the universe who expressed through him his love for sinners. The nine Jewish lepers represented the attitude of the spiritual leaders of Israel. They never returned to Jesus to thank God for their physical healing. They did not realize that their physical healing was only a shadow of the spiritual healing that they truly needed. They could have been healed spiritually if they had placed their faith in Jesus as their Messiah. From this story it appears that at least one physically healed man, who was thankful to God and his Son Jesus, became a true son of Abraham. He placed his faith in God and acknowledged Jesus as the Son of God, the Master of his body, soul and spirit. And again, this man was a foreigner!

Just before Christmas one year, I recall Eff Martin (one

of the elders at Menlo Park Presbyterian Church) teaching the congregation from Isaiah 9 about the prophecy of our coming Lord in which Jesus is referred to as "Wonderful Counselor." Eff gave an invitation to the congregation to seriously consider inviting Jesus into their lives, saying that He would become *their* Wonderful Counselor. The following week, he got a phone call from some friends who had invited a young man to church that morning. As he listened to that sermon of hope, salvation and peace, he invited Jesus into his life and spent Sunday afternoon with his friends rejoicing over the love of God and his gift of salvation. When I heard about this it reminded me of Paul's words to the church of Thessalonica: "Rejoice always; pray without ceasing; in everything give thanks; for this is God's will for you in Christ Jesus" (1 Thessalonians 5:16-18).

To be called a disciple of Jesus Christ is a high calling. When we confess him as our Lord, he begins to bring us into spiritual maturity so that we can join him in his wonderful plan of evangelism—"seeking to save those who are lost." That ministry of redemption occurs in the midst of a spiritual battlefield. Our Lord encourages and commands his disciples to love our lives, our families and our possessions less, and to love him more.

Further, he commands that we do not become stumbling blocks to those who are on their way to the Lord. He commands that we prepare our hearts to be ready to rebuke and forgive our repentant brothers and sisters. He commands that we continue to grow in our faith towards Christ so that his will in heaven may be accomplished on earth through us. He also commands that we minister as his disciples with hearts of thankfulness because of the grace and spiritual healing he demonstrated towards us when we placed our faith in him as Lord and Savior, and that we depend on the indwelling Holy Spirit to empower us to obey His commands.

APPENDIX

My life has been rich with discipleship opportunities. And although each group has had its own special characteristics, the common thread among them all has been hearts willing to be *equipped for the work of ministry* (Ephesians 4:11-13).

It always begins with prayer. I ask the Lord to bring into my life believers whose hearts have been opened by Him, who are ready for discipleship. Then, as you have already read in the previous Discipleship 101-104 papers, I open the gospels to show them how Jesus, after speaking to his Father, went about calling out people from all walks of life, saying to them: *"Follow me and I will make you to become fishers of men"* (Mark 1:17).

The following pages contain materials compiled over the years with the help of many faithful brothers and sisters to develop what has come to be known as ***The Timothy Discipleship Experience***, which in contrast to a program, is a lifestyle of discipleship and not just a group study.

In your going, make disciples…
This is a study of our risen Lord's final words to his disciples, just before he returned to heaven in all his glory and power.

The Timothy Discipleship Experience
This is a written covenant I have developed over the years that helps potential disciples to understand the beginning, middle and end of our commitment, both to the Lord and to each other, as well as the time we will be together *(each group typically runs 12-18 months)*. After they have taken some time to read over the covenant and pray about their involvement, I then invite them to a first meeting. This is when I answer any questions they may have about continuing their commitment to the group. The group is actually "formed" the next week with those who decide to return to begin the adventure of *becoming fishers of men*. (A template containing the "Covenant" is provided. This is a sample to get you started, or that will at least give you some ideas for writing your own.) Also included is a sample of a weekly *Timothy* meeting. Of course, each group will be different and leadership styles will vary.

The Timothys
Included are some testimonies from two groups I recently discipled, which I hope will be a source of encouragement and motivation for you to begin your own group. As of this writing, I have joined four former Timothys who have begun two new groups.

Pass The Torch
This is a message based on 2 Timothy 2:1-10 that I give to those who have completed their commitment to *The Timothy Discipleship Experience* with the hope that they will spend the rest of their lives discipling all those who the Lord brings to them until He comes again.

Discipleship paper by Steve Hixon

Inductive Study Method
Material was taken from the study guide *Free At Last! The New Covenant*. Included is the introduction to that study guide, the principles behind the inductive study method, and for practice, the first two chapters of the study guide itself.

May our risen and glorified Lord and Savior richly bless you in the days ahead as you seek, by the power of the Holy Spirit, to begin to help God's people *become equipped for the work of ministry*.

The Fishing Boat

by Rodd Ritchie

The boat that you see is about You and Me.
Memories of Half Moon Bay,
large vessels all around, fishing off the dock,
waiting for the catch.

Memories of San Francisco,
Christmas by the Bay;
the sight of fishing boats,
the smell of crab and ocean breeze.

Memories to come of fishing in St. Auygulf.*

The boat is a gift to the one who taught me to be a fisher of men.

I am the little boat you see, ready to be lowered down; taught by a faithful servant,
hoping to catch the Kingdom full, ready to receive the crown.

Merry Christmas--
Your Son, Rodd

Our sons, Ron and Rodd, were raised near the beaches and boat harbor of a fleet of fishing vessels in Half Moon Bay, CA. The boat above is a model of one of those deep sea fishing vessels. Rodd presented me with the model and poem as a Christmas gift in 1999.

After high school, Rodd went on to Westmont College in Santa Barbara, and then moved to Boise, ID and began preparation for ministry at Cole Community Church by participating in a three year program at their Biblical Training Center. He is now on staff as a co-pastor and elder.

Rodd married Kyna Swanson, whom he met at Westmont College, and they are the proud parents of three sons: Caleb, Joshua and Alex.

*St. Auygulf is a small fishing village on the shores of the southern coast of France where we vacationed for several years during summer months.

"In your going, make disciples..."

Matthew 28:16-20

By Ron R. Ritchie

Dr. John R.W. Stott is rector emeritus of All Souls Church in London, England, and now carries on a worldwide teaching ministry, both in person and through his many books. He has also had a great influence on the student world through his relationship with InterVarsity ministry. As a result of his worldwide travels, he recently wrote a very challenging statement to the leaders of the Church of Jesus Christ in an article entitled *"The Great Need for Making Disciples."* He wrote:

> The numbers of people coming to Christ around the world are staggering. Today we are witnessing perhaps one of the greatest expansions of the Church worldwide, especially in the Two-Thirds World. These numbers would suggest great success stories—that the mission of the Church is being accomplished. And yet, very reputable and deeply committed church leaders from Two-Thirds World countries are quick to note that the Church is exploding with extraordinary numerical growth *without depth*. We are witnessing one of the most *over-evangelized*, but *under discipled* eras in history.[1]

Dr. Stott has challenged the minds and hearts of Christian leaders round the world to take another look at the words of our risen Lord, which he spoke to his eleven disciples just before he returned to heaven. Those words form what we now call "The Great Commission," which may cause many of us to either refocus, at the very least, reconsider our ministries.

The Great Commission

But the eleven disciples proceeded to Galilee, to the mountain which Jesus had designated. When they saw Him, they worshiped Him; but some were doubtful. And Jesus came up and spoke to them, saying, "All authority has been given to Me in heaven and on earth. "Go therefore and make disciples of all the nations, baptizing them in the name of the Father and the Son and the Holy Spirit, teaching them to observe all that I commanded you; and lo, I am with you always, even to the end of the age." (Matthew 28:16-20, NASB)

First Century Context: As you may recall, Jesus had said to his disciples in the upper room in Jerusalem: "…after I have been raised, I will go ahead of you to Galilee" (Matthew 26:32). Galilee was home for most of the disciples, and by going there after the events at the cross they were safe from the ever-present religious and political forces around the temple area. Then once the disciples faithfully arrived in Galilee, he appeared to seven of them on the shores of the Sea of Galilee, and over a breakfast of love that he prepared for them, Jesus challenged Peter's love for him and then encouraged him: "Shepherd My sheep" (see John 21:1-19). Then our risen Lord appeared to the eleven disciples on a mountain slope and gave them their commission for ministry within the age of the Spirit. This occurred between the events of Luke 24:43-44.

---

[1]Meriti Sawyer - In the Gap, *The Research and Development of the Church*, John Stott Ministries, p. 1, Dec. 02 – emphasis mine.

At that meeting, the disciples were filled with mixed emotions. For some it was a time to worship the risen Lord as their Messiah, the Son of God and King, while for others it was a time of struggle because of their doubtful hearts. By this time, it's likely that Thomas, Peter, and John no longer doubted what they were seeing and experiencing, but nevertheless some still did. They had seen him, touched him, and even eaten with their wonderful, risen Lord, yet they were still having a hard time getting used to him in his full glory as the Risen Son of God. They were in the process of becoming mature.

A. *"All authority has been given to Me in heaven and on earth."* When Jesus walked the earth in human form, his authority was limited as he submitted to the will of his Father: "...He humbled Himself by becoming obedient to the point of death, even death on a cross" (Philippians 2:8). He had lived his short life on this earth for the will of his Father. But after his death and resurrection, Paul tells us in Philippians 2:9-11 that his Father "...highly exalted Him, and bestowed on Him the name which is above every name, that at the name of Jesus every knee should bow, of those who are in heaven, and on earth, and under the earth..."

After his resurrection, Jesus was given unlimited power and authority over sickness and death, over political and religious powers, and over what was both visible and invisible—*"world forces of this darkness and spiritual forces of wickedness in the heavenly places"* (Ephesians 6:12). And since he had been given all authority over the visible and invisible universe as the one and only sovereign Lord, he continued to offer redemption to the world, *"...to seek and to save that which was lost"* (Luke 19:10). The disciples needed to be assured of this spiritual reality when they were given their commission to move out into the fallen and devilish world with this message of redemption.

B. *"Go therefore* [in my authority]..." The Greek verb translates, *"In your going,"* or *"Having gone."* In this phrase, evangelism is assumed. *"...And make disciples..."* In this phrase, "make disciples" is not a suggestion but a command. This is the heart of our Lord's great commission.

In the very beginning of Jesus' ministry on the shores of the Sea of Galilee, we find him walking along the beach. He calls out to two local fishermen, Simon and his brother Andrew, who were casting a net into the sea. And Jesus said to them, "'Follow Me, and I will make you become fishers of men.' Immediately they left their nets and followed Him" (Mark 1:17-18). He then invited James and John to follow him (see Mark 1:19-20), and soon he had twelve men.

Upon calling these men to follow him, Jesus began the process of making them his disciples so that when he left this earth and returned to his Father, the same wonderful message of redemption would continue through them until he returned to set up his kingdom. He encouraged those men with words like,"If you abide in My word, then you are truly disciples of Mine..." (John 8:31). "By this all men will know that you are My disciples, if you have love for one another" (John 13:35). "By this is My father glorified, that you bear much fruit, and so prove to be My disciples" (John 15:8).

When the disciples began to preach the gospel of Jesus Christ, the message of spiritual redemption, God moved the hearts of the listeners to place their faith in his Son as their Lord and Savior. Once those new believers declared their faith in Jesus as their Lord, the disciples were commanded to spend time with them to *"make disciples"* of them, to teach and prepare them to walk in the truth of their new Lord in the same manner he had taught them. It was the difference between giving them a fish and actually teaching them how to fish on their own.

"...of all the nations..." During Jesus' ministry on earth, there had been times when he had given his disciples authority over unclean spirits and diseases and sickness, but at those times he told them, "Do not go in the way of the Gentiles, and do not enter any city of the Samaritans; but rather go to the lost sheep of the house of Israel" (Matthew 10:5-6). But once Israel had rejected their King and Messiah, the resurrected Lord set his

disciples free to go into the whole world and to preach the gospel of Jesus Christ to the Gentiles, as well as the Jews.

Recently I met a young Christian who told me, "I belong to a church where I can't get anyone to disciple me. I went to my pastor, and he had no time for me. I'm frustrated, because I have a hunger to teach, and the education director gave me a class, but I don't know what I'm doing. Every week when I show up I'm terrified with the tension between wanting to teach and not knowing how. Can you help me?" Pastor-teachers are called by God *"to equip the saints for the work of the ministry"* (see Ephesians 4:1-11). That process involves an appeal not only to the heart, but to the will and the mind. Paul, in writing to one of his disciples, Timothy, gives us a concise description of this process: "The things which you have heard from me in the presence of many witnesses, entrust these to faithful men [and women] who will be able to teach others also" (2 Timothy 2:2).

C. *"...Baptizing them in the name of the Father and the Son and the Holy Spirit."* As new believers came into the spiritual body of Jesus Christ, our risen Lord instructed his disciples to publicly baptize them (dip them in water) as a physical symbol—something they could feel—of the inner spiritual reality: Being identified with our Lord's death, burial, and resurrection (see Romans 6). This physical witness of baptism would clearly identify them publicly as disciples of Jesus Christ. It was to be a one-time spiritual and physical experience. (Note: The new believers were to be baptized in the name, not name*s*, of the Father and Son and Holy Spirit, showing the oneness of the triune God.)

D. *"...Teaching them to observe all that I commanded you..."* A disciple can teach a new believer only what he or she has been taught and what he or she obeys. Jesus taught his disciples the facts about three relationships: **1)** His relationship with his Father: *"...I am in the Father, and the Father in Me..."* (John 14:11); **2)** His relationship with them: *"This is My commandment, that you love one another, just as I have loved you"* (John 15:12); and, **3)** His relationship with the enemy: *"...that through death He might render powerless him who had the power of death, that is, the devil..."* (Hebrews 2:14).

At Peninsula Bible Church, where I served the Lord for some 27 years, the elders and under-shepherds are all encouraged to take time, in addition to their many other responsibilities, to disciple other men and women and to teach them to observe all that Christ has commanded them. Once those disciples become spiritually mature, they, in turn, are then encouraged to gather together other men and women from the body and disciple them. In both the private and public teaching of their curriculum they have the same three themes: **(1)** The New Covenant, which is about our love relationship with God; **(2)** Body Life, which is all about our love relationship with each other; and, **(3)** Spiritual Warfare, which is about our relationship with our spiritual enemy who was defeated at the Cross.

Dallas Willard wrote: "As a disciple of Jesus I am with him by choice and by grace, learning from him how to live in the kingdom of God...his life flowing through mine. I am learning from Jesus to live my life as he would live his life if he were I. I am not necessarily learning to do everything he did, but I am learning how to do everything I do in the manner that he did all that he did. ("The Divine Conspiracy", p. 283)

E. *"...Lo [remember], I am [present tense] **with you always** [now and forever], **even to the end of the age."** By this statement, Jesus meant that because all authority had been given to him by his Father (since he was raised to glory in his new resurrected body), he is now present with all of those who minister by his power and in his name until the end of the age—until he comes again. Jesus is no longer limited to where he can be at any given moment in time. He can be with all of us at once, wherever we are. He will never leave us or forsake us. At times he will be visible and at times he will be invisible, but we are not to fear because he will always be present.

A great example of this spiritual reality happened to the apostle Paul some 18 years after the Lord's Ascension. The apostle had moved into the wicked city of Corinth on his second missionary journey. At one point he became so fearful that our risen Lord appeared to him in a vision and said, "Do not be afraid any longer, but go on speaking and do not be silent; for I am with you, and no man will attack you in order to harm you, for I have many people in this city" (Acts 18:9-11). This is a wonderful encouragement for us, for no matter what situations we get into as followers of Jesus Christ, the Lord, who used to be limited in his humanity on this earth and could only be with his twelve or so at any one time, can now be with each one of us. But he also promises us that he will never leave us. We are never alone. And in that intimacy he protects us, guides us, instructs us and he is willing to meet whatever our needs are present at that moment.

In light of the clear command of our risen and glorified Lord and Savior Jesus Christ, it seems appropriate to ask ourselves a most important question: "What plans have we made or what plans are we making to prepare ourselves to obey His command and to participate in his plan to *go...and make disciples of all the nations...*? May our risen and ever present Lord Jesus richly bless each of us as we seek, by the power the indwelling Holy Spirit, to obey him in this most adventurous ministry in this present day.

"All authority has been given to Me in heaven and on earth. Go therefore and make disciples of all the nations, baptizing them in the name of the Father and the Son and the Holy Spirit, teaching them to observe all that I commanded you; and lo, I am with you always, even to the end of the age." (Matthew 28:16-20, NASB)

℘ ℂ

Rest

by St. Augustine

"...Thou hast made us for thyself and restless is our heart until it comes to rest in thee."

A man wants to praise you, man who is only a small portion of what you have created and who goes about carrying with him his own mortality, the evidence of his own sin, and evidence that resists the proud... Yet still man, this small portion of creation, wants to praise you. You stimulate him to take pleasure in praising you, because you have made us for yourself, and our hearts are restless until they find rest in you.

Confessions of St. Augustine, an excerpt from Christian History Magazine, Vol. 6, No. 3, p. 16.

The Timothy Discipleship Experience

> The title, *The Timothy Discipleship Experience*, denotes that we will seek to
> live out the same daily life of Jesus as He related to his disciples, community
> and world and is, therefore, more than just a weekly fellowship group, a
> home Bible study or a classroom commitment.

The Historical Background

Jesus was a disciple of His Heavenly Father. The prophet Isaiah (740-681 BC), who also was a discipler (8:16), wrote of some of the characteristics of the coming Messiah:

The Lord GOD has given Me the tongue of *disciples*, that I may know how to sustain the weary one with a word He awakens Me morning by morning, He awakens My ear to listen *as a disciple*. The Lord GOD has opened My ear; and I was not disobedient nor did I turn back. (Isaiah 50:4-5, *emphasis mine*)

Jesus chose twelve disciples (30 AD). "As He was going along by the Sea of Galilee, He saw Simon and Andrew, the brother of Simon, casting a net in the sea; for they were fishermen. And Jesus said to them, *'Follow Me, and I will make you become fishers of men.'* Immediately they left their nets and followed Him. Going on a little farther, He saw James the son of Zebedee, and John his brother, who were also in the boat mending the nets. Immediately He called them; and they left their father Zebedee in the boat with the hired servants, and went away to follow Him" (Mark 1:16-20). "And He went up on the mountain and summoned those whom He Himself wanted, and they came to Him. And He appointed twelve so that they would be with Him and that He could send them out to preach…" (Mark 3:13-14).

Jesus, our resurrected Lord, *commanded* his disciples (33 AD). "All authority has been given to Me in heaven and on earth. Go therefore and *make disciples* of all the nations, baptizing them in the name of the Father and the Son and the Holy Spirit, teaching them to observe all that I commanded you; and lo, I am with you always, even to the end of the age" (Matthew 28:18-20).

The apostle Paul discipled Timothy. On Paul's second missionary journey (50-52 AD), he "…came to Derbe and then to Lystra (cities located in south central Turkey) where a disciple named Timothy (Greek: *"God honoring one"* - Acts 16:1) lived, whose mother was a Jewess and a believer, but whose father was a Greek. (Timothy became a Christian during Paul's first missionary journey to this region in 46-47 AD). Timothy joined Paul as his faithful companion until his death in 67 AD. Just before the apostle's death he wrote to his beloved spiritual son and said: "You therefore, my son, be strong in the grace that is in Christ Jesus. The things which you have heard from me in the presence of many witnesses, entrust these to faithful men who will be able to teach others also" (2 Timothy 2:1-2).

Our *Risen* Lord Jesus Calls and Commands each New Generation
to go and *make disciples* of all nations

Howard Hendricks, in his book, *Iron Sharpens Iron*, said: "Jesus' command to his followers to *'go and make disciples of all nations'* is distinctive in that Jesus remains the Master, the Discipler. He wants people who are recruited to the faith to remain *His* disciples, *His* learners."

Disciple: Greek: *mathetes*, a learner accomplished by endeavor, a pupil,
an adherent, an imitator of their teacher (John 8:31).
W.E. Vine, *An Expository Dictionary of Biblical Words,* p. 171.

So, what is *the goal* of *The Timothy Discipleship Experience*?

To *make disciples* denotes a process that takes place over a period of time, as illustrated in the life of Jesus. The discipleship process is designed to help spiritually maturing believers continue their growth in the wisdom and grace of our Lord Jesus. Spiritually maturing believers are those who are willing to learn how to move from a place of depending on themselves and others, to becoming totally dependent on the Lord Jesus and His Spirit for their spiritual walk within the body of Christ, and in the world around them. Paul wrote to the Colossians: "I have become its [the Church] servant by the commission God gave me to present to you the word of God in its fullness—the mystery that has been kept hidden for ages and generations, but is now disclosed to the saints. To them God has chosen to make known among the Gentiles the glorious riches of this mystery, which is Christ in you, the hope of glory. We proclaim him, admonishing and teaching everyone with all wisdom, so that we may present everyone perfect [spiritually mature] in Christ." (Colossians 1:25-28)

What are some *Steps* that will help one accomplish this goal?

1. We will spend time building a **mutual relationship of love**. (1 Thessalonians 2:7-9)
2. We will experience a time of **mutual prayer**. (1 Thessalonians 5:17, 25)
3. We will experience a time of **mutual study and teaching of the Word**. (Matthew 28:18-20)
4. We will experience a time of **mutual evaluation of our lives**. (Luke 22:31-32)
5. We will seek opportunities to **pass on our experiences to others**. (2 Timothy 2:1-2)

What are some of the *Areas of Study*?

1. The Principles of Discipleship. "Then the eleven disciples went to Galilee, to the mountain where Jesus had told them to go. When they saw him, they worshiped him; but some doubted. Then Jesus came to them and said, 'All authority in heaven and on earth has been given to me. Therefore go and make disciples of all nations, baptizing them in the name of the Father and of the Son and of the Holy Spirit, and teaching them to obey everything I have commanded you. And surely I am with you always, to the very end of the age.'" (Matthew 28:16-20, NIV)

2. The Principles of Inductive Bible Study. "Do your best to present yourself to God as one approved, a workman who does not need to be ashamed and who correctly handles the word of truth." (2 Timothy 2:15,)

a. **The New Covenant** *(our relationship with God)*. "This is the covenant I will make with the house of Israel after that time," declares the LORD. "I will put my law in their minds and write it on their hearts. I will be their God, and they will be my people. No longer will a man teach his neighbor, or a man his brother, saying, 'Know the LORD,' because they will all know me, from the least of them to the greatest," declares the LORD. "For I will forgive their wickedness and will remember their sins no more." (Jer. 31:33-34; Heb. 8-9)

b. **Spiritual Warfare** (our relationship with God's enemy). "Finally, be strong in the Lord and in his mighty power. Put on the full armor of God so that you can take your stand against the devil's schemes. For our struggle is not against flesh and blood, but against the rulers, against the authorities, against the powers of this dark world and against the spiritual forces of evil in the heavenly realms. Therefore put on the full armor of God, so that when the day of evil comes, you may be able to stand your ground, and after you have done everything, to stand. Stand firm then, with the belt of truth buckled around your waist, with the breastplate of righteousness in place, and with your feet fitted with the readiness that comes from the gospel of peace. In addition to all this, take up the shield of faith, with which you can extinguish all the flaming arrows of the evil one. Take the helmet of salvation and the sword of the Spirit, which is the word of God. And pray in the Spirit on all occasions with all kinds of prayers and requests. With this in mind, be alert and always keep on praying for all the saints." (Ephesians 6:10-18)

    c.   <u>Body Life</u> (our relationships within our spiritual family). "As the Father has loved me, so have I loved you. Now remain in my love. If you obey my commands, you will remain in my love, just as I have obeyed my Father's commands and remain in his love. I have told you this so that my joy may be in you and that your joy may be complete. My command is this: Love each other as I have loved you. Greater love has no one than this, that he lay down his life for his friends." (John 15:9-13; Acts 2:41-47)

    3. The Principles of Spiritual Counseling: "He went to Nazareth, where he had been brought up, and on the Sabbath day he went into the synagogue, as was his custom. And he stood up to read. The scroll of the prophet Isaiah was handed to him. Unrolling it, he found the place where it is written: 'The Spirit of the Lord is on me, because he has anointed me to preach good news to the poor. He has sent me to proclaim freedom for the prisoners and recovery of sight for the blind, to release the oppressed, to proclaim the year of the Lord's favor.'" (Luke 4:16-19, NIV.)

    4. The Principles of Defending our Hope: **"But in your hearts set apart Christ as Lord. Always be prepared to give an answer to everyone who asks you to give the reason for the hope that you have. But do this with gentleness and respect…"** (1 Peter 3:15)

    5. The Major Doctrines of God as found in His Word: Shortly after the crucifixion, Jesus met two discouraged disciples on the road to Emmaus but they did not recognize him, still believing he was dead and buried. Jesus addressed their problem, saying to them, "'How foolish you are, and how slow of heart to believe all that the prophets have spoken! Did not the Christ have to suffer these things and then enter his glory?' And beginning with Moses and all the Prophets, he explained to them what was said in all the Scriptures concerning himself…When he was at the table with them, he took bread, gave thanks, broke it and began to give it to them. Then their eyes were opened and they recognized him, and he disappeared from their sight. They asked each other, 'Were not our hearts burning within us while he talked with us on the road and opened the Scriptures to us?'" (Luke 24:25-27; 30-32)

    "All Scripture is God-breathed and is useful for teaching, rebuking, correcting and training in righteousness, so that the [person] of God may be thoroughly equipped for every good work." (2 Timothy 3:16-17)

What kind of *Relationship* will we have with one another?

Calling [the disciples] to Himself, Jesus said to them, "You know that those who are recognized as rulers of the Gentiles lord it over them; and their great men exercise authority over them. But it is not this way among you, but whoever wishes to become great among you shall be your servant; and whoever wishes to be first among you shall be slave of all. *For even the Son of Man did not come to be served, but to serve, and to give His life a ransom for many.*" (Mark 10:42-45, *emphasis mine*. Also, see Matthew 23:8-12.)

When do we begin *The Timothy Discipleship Experience?*

We will not begin until you have prayed about this invitation for a few weeks. The reason behind this statement is found in the requirements: *Discipleship* means a season of disciplines (2 Timothy 2:15); a word of commitment that will not be broken (Matthew 5:37); as well as a season of hard work outside of and as part of our meetings (Luke 9:57-62). There will be approximately five (5) hours of homework before we meet each week and then, we will be together for approximately four (4) hours of prayer, study, and sharing our lives with one another. After the meeting each week we will share a meal together either at our meeting place or in a local restaurant in order to develop our fellowship with each other and the world around us. *Please keep in mind that this is not a fellowship group, a home bible study, or a normal classroom experience. Our model is the daily life of Jesus and how he related to his disciples.* This experience is not something you add on to your already busy schedule, so pray about paring down your current schedule.

Reading Material:

Foundations of the Christian Faith .... by James Montgomery Boice
The Master Plan of Evangelism .... by Robert Coleman
In the Name of Jesus .... by Henri J. M. Nouwen
Baptism and Fullness .... by John R.W. Stott
Talking With My Father .... by Ray C. Stedman
Free at Last! .... by Ron R. Ritchie
The Case for Christ .... by Lee Strobel
The Case for Faith .... by Lee Strobel
The Great Omission .... by Dallas Willard

(You will also be required to buy a set of *Tool Books* that will prepare you to become a *fisher of men*.)

The Timothy Discipleship Experience **is a 12-18 month commitment to Jesus Christ and each other.**

We plan to meet weekly on _____ evenings from ___ PM to ___ PM for _____ months, beginning on _____, 200__. Our group will meet at _____ _____.

A Time to Pray: Please pray about this open door of opportunity for a few weeks. Within that prayer, we want you to ask God to continue to make you a faithful person so that in time you will be able *to disciple others for the rest of your life* on this earth. We also want you to make a commitment to your Lord and Savior Jesus Christ so that once you begin this experience you will choose to remain faithful to the Lord Jesus and to the *Timothy group* until our season of study is completed. (2 Timothy 2:13, Luke 9:57-62)

When you have decided to join the *Timothy group* please call us at: _____

"If anyone wishes to come after Me, he must deny himself, and take up his cross daily and follow Me. For whoever wishes to save his life will lose it, but whoever loses his life for My sake, he is the one who will save it. For what is a man profited if he gains the whole world, and loses or forfeits himself?" (Luke 9:23-25) *Jesus, to his disciples*

"You therefore, my son, be strong in the grace that is in Christ Jesus. The things which you have heard from me in the presence of many witnesses, entrust these to faithful men who will be able to teach others also." (2 Timothy 2:1-2) *Paul, to his spiritual son and disciple Timothy*

Sample of a Typical
Timothy Discipleship Experience Meeting

We meet weekly at someone's home, or in a business or church conference room for 2-3 hours, and then we go out to dinner together (another couple of hours).

1.   We will spend time building a mutual relationship of love. (1 Thessalonians 2:7-9)

Depending on how many disciples are in the group, the first evening together is spent sharing our personal histories, along with photos of our families. We are then free to ask questions of each other. Personally, these times have turned out to be most rewarding to me. It is also at this first meeting that we gather contact information for a "roster" so we can check in on one another as the Spirit moves our hearts. Oftentimes, members make plans to meet individually for breakfasts, lunches or dinners with each other during the week for fellowship, counseling, or to plan future events together. Likewise, if someone is sick, out of town, or late, we call each other so that all of us know where everyone is in any given week.

The Timothys will serve one another by taking on various responsibilities to facilitate group meetings as well. This can include writing down prayer requests, gathering information for the roster, sending reminder emails, planning events, ordering books, etc. It should also include leading group discussions on various topics such the Biblical text, assigned books, etc.

2.   We will experience a time of mutual prayer. (1 Thessalonians. 5:17, 25)

Each week we share our prayer requests with the group. Someone in the group will volunteer to write them down, including the date we prayed, and then later fill in the date our Lord answered some of those requests. We also take the prayer requests to dinner and pray for them just before we adjourn. Finally, we take a *group photo* as soon as possible and give a copy of the photo to each person as a daily reminder to pray for one another.

3.   We will experience a time of mutual study and teaching of the Word. (Matthew 28:18-20)

We agree to study either one of the gospel accounts or one of the New Testament epistles. Whether it is the Gospel of John, the Letters to the Corinthians, or perhaps Paul's letter to the Ephesians, we use the Inductive Bible Study Method. (A sample is provided at the end of this Discipleship manual – see the Appendix. The sample was taken from my inductive study guide *Free At Last!*) Each week a homework assignment is given, which would include a portion of the Biblical text we are studying, along with reading from other materials that compliment our Biblical study. It may also include study of a particular "word" or "phrase" that would then be shared with the group.

The following is an example of a weekly reminder concerning an upcoming Timothy meeting:

For our next meeting on Tuesday, May 24ᵗʰ at 6:15 PM, please complete the following:

(1) Read the book, "In the Name of Jesus," by Henri Nouwen, in one sitting. Bill M. will lead us in a discussion of that book.
(2) Continue your inductive study in "The New Covenant Workbook" up to 2 Corinthians 3:6.
(3) Look up the many biblical references concerning "The New Covenant" and be able to explain it in your own words. (Use your Bible Concordance)

Rick will be out this week due to an evening business meeting at his company. Keep him in prayer.

The Timothys are expected to spend a minimum of five (5) hours of study per week on the assigned material before returning to the next meeting. As leaders, we continue to try and show the Timothy's the three main areas of the truth of God: *the New Covenant* (our relationship with God); *Body Life* (our relationship with each other); and, *Spiritual Warfare* (our relationship with Satan, who is continually seeking to destroy the other two relationships!). These truths are clearly seen in the Paul's letter to the Ephesians. Once the group has completed the inductive study, they are then taught how to teach other disciples. This includes learning to put a message together, and then how to present it to others (see the following outline for a message on Elijah from 1 Kings).

4.   We will experience a time of mutual evaluation of our lives. (Luke 22:31-32)

During our sharing times either at the beginning of our meetings or at dinner, the Timothys will often ask for feedback concerning their families, their work, their community activities, etc. We have always sought to make that time a "safe place" to share one's heart, hopes and dreams, as well as our personal struggles without the fear of violating each other's confidence. Those times also become what one would call "a teachable moment" not only for the one who shared, but for the rest of us as well. We try to keep each other *thinking God's thoughts after Him.*

5.   We will seek opportunities to pass on our experiences to others. (2 Timothy 2:1-2)

As disciplers, we are always looking for open doors of opportunity where we can share a ministry together. We have taken ministry trips with our interns and Timothys to Holland, Germany, France, Italy, Switerland, Spain, Greece and Turkey, as well as Israel, Eygpt and Nigeria. There have been open doors to minister in the Philippines, Indonesia, Malaysia, Singapore, Japan, China, Austrailia, the island of Taiwan, and in Pakistan. We have ministered in the prisons of Columbia, Mexico and in the United States. And, speaking of the U.S., we have traveled with teams of men and women to almost every state, and over the years have visited a host of college campuses, not to mention hundreds of restaurants filled with folks open to hearing the Gospel of Jesus Christ. We have worked together in homeless shelters, food lines for the poor, and "assisted living" homes. Those times are invaluable as we seek to invite the Holy Spirit (living within us) to make the invisible Jesus (who also lives within in) visible.

6.   We share a meal together and the sweet aroma of Christ with those around us.

We usually find a local restaurant that we will return to weekly, where we can get to know the restaurant owner/manager, the servers, and possibly some of the more frequent customers. We want to bring the *sweet aroma of Christ* to those all around us (2 Corinthians 2:14-16). One of our groups had the privilege of presenting to our faithful Mexican waiter a Bible with his name inscribed in gold letters. He responded by saying: "A Bible, I have always wanted one. Thank you so very much!"

My son Ron, also a former Timothy, had built a relationship with our French waiter at the restaurant where our group was meeting regularly. During that time, Ron became engaged to Sylvia and they invited both the waiter and his son to their wedding. Another time, while we were all eating at a local fish market, one of the young college girls serving another section came to us with tears in her eyes and asked: "Are you the guys who pray?" (She and the other servers had seen us together many times, and noticed us praying together before we would leave the restaurant each week.) We said, "Yes," and she asked, "Do you mind praying for my boyfriend who dove into the pool at Stanford University and we think he has broken his neck." We pulled out a chair and asked her to join us. We all prayed for her boyfriend's full recovery. She thanked us and returned to work. The following week she found us again and with a thankful heart, told us that her boyfriend had fully recovered from his accident.

Our Timothy groups have had many opportunities to develop some very deep bonds with those who have served us over the years in a variety of local restaurants. It has become so obvious that meeting at a restaurant is really *not* about the food. It's about loving, in the name of Christ, those who have served us.

Summary: Each week will truly be a new adventure as we allow the Holy Spirit full control of our lives, our plans, our hopes and our dreams. So, ***just show up*** and enjoy the adventure as He seeks to make the invisible Jesus, who lives within us, visible to those around us!

Sample Format for Preaching and Teaching

Title: *The Cure for Depression* (1 Kings 19:1-21). [Pick a title that sums up the passage. It can be a question, a statement, a challenge or an encouragement.]

Opening Remarks: Try to find a modern illustration out of your own life, or some current event that will help your audience connect with the passage of scripture you are teaching. [Look for the illustration _after_ you have finished all of your *inductive* work and have drawn out some *spiritual principles* within the passage. The illustration should not be the driving force behind the teaching. Rather, it should come from the passage of scripture itself.]

Transition into the passage: Move from your opening illustration by letting your audience know where you plan to take them. Then, give them a brief overview of your outline.

Outline: *The Cure for Depression*   1 Kings 19:1-21
       1. **Don't lose sight of the Presence of God**   **19: 1-8**
       2. **Don't lose sight of the Love of God**   **19: 9-14**
       3. **Don't lose sight of the Sovereignty of God**   **19:15-21**

Transition: Move your audience from the outline to the main subject, and then into the first part of your outline:

1. **Don't lose sight of the *Presence* of God**   **1 Kings 19:1-8**
   - a. Read the passage: 1 Kings 19:1-8
   - b. Keep the prophet Elijah and the passage in its 875-848 B.C. historical context.
   - c. Explain the meaning of the passage in its 8th century context.
   - d. Pull out the spiritual principles (based on 2 Timothy 3:16-17)
   - e. Give a contemporary illustration to help make the truth more personally relevant to your audience.

Transition: *The Cure for Depression* is not losing sight of the presence of God.

2. **Don't lose sight of the *Love* of God**   **1 Kings 19:9-14**
   - a. Read the passage: 1 Kings 19:9-14
   - b. Keep the prophet Elijah and the passage in its 875-848 B.C. historical context.
   - c. Explain the meaning of the passage in its 8th century context.
   - d. Pull out the spiritual principles (based on 2 Timothy 3:16-17)
   - e. Give a contemporary illustration to help make the truth more personally relevant to your audience.

Transition: *Refer back to the title,* **The Cure for Depression** is not losing sight of the presence and love of God

3. **Don't lose sight of the *Sovereignty* of God**   **1 Kings 19:15-21**
   - a. Read the passage: 1 Kings 19:15-21
   - b. Keep the prophet Elijah and the passage in its 875-848 B.C. historical context.
   - c. Explain the meaning of the passage in its 8th century context.
   - d. Pull out the spiritual principles (based on 2 Timothy 3:16-17)
   - e. Give a contemporary illustration to help make the truth more personally relevant to your audience.

Summarize: *The Cure for Depression* can be ours when we…***don't lose sight of** the **Presence**, the **Love** and the Sovereignty of God.*

Application: So what? How does this apply to me today?
      Close with an illustration based on personal experience, a current event or the experience of a friend, ***who placed their faith in God to cure their depression.***

A Word of Encouragement
from recent Timothys

The letters on the following pages include testimonies from the last two groups I had the privilege of discipling, along with Norm Nason, a local businessman and former Timothy and now an elder at Saratoga Federated in Saratoga, California. We hope their words will be a source of encouragement and motivation for you as you begin to pray about starting your own group of disciples.

I recently received the following email from two of my former Timothys, Don Ott and Mark Campbell, regarding a converation they had with my discipling professor at Dallas Seminary (1964-1966):

"Mark Cambell and I went to a workshop sponsored by the Evangelical Free Church, primarily to have a day of being taught by Dr. Howard Hendricks (who is now in his 80's). We decided we would introduce ourselves to him before the meeting started. After telling him our names, we added: *We're your grandkids. We're in Ron Ritchie's Timothy group.* Dr. Hendricks was pleased to hear that, and after saying a few nice things about you, he paused and smiled a little impishly. *When you see Ron again,* Prof said, *Would you let him know I just got six more men myself.*"

Mentoring vs. Discipleship

by Howard and William Hendricks

*What is the difference between mentoring and discipleship?
They are closely related but not exactly the same. Both involve*
instruction *based on* relationship.

*...Discipleship involves a call, a direct invitation from the teacher that borders on a
command ... Jesus told the fishermen Peter and Andrew,* "'Come, follow me," Jesus said,
'and I will make you fishers of men.' At once they left their nets and followed him"
(Matthew 4:19-20). *Then, he ran into their colleagues, James and John. Again,* "Jesus
called them, and immediately they left the boat and their father and followed him"
(Matthew 4:21-22). *The same pattern was repeated with the rest of the twelve.*

*The word "disciple" means "learner." In Jesus' day, teachers roamed the ancient world
recruiting bands of "learners" who then followed these masters and adopted their
teaching. Sometimes the disciples became masters themselves and developed their own
followings. But Jesus' command to his followers to* "go and make disciples of all nations"
(Matthew 28:16-20) *is distinctive in that Jesus remains the Master, the Discipler. He
wants people who are recruited to the faith to remain his disciples, his learners.*
Discipleship, *as we know it today, tends to narrow its focus to the spiritual dimension.
Ideally, it should touch every area of life—our personal life and lifestyle, our work, our
relationships. But* **discipleship** *always looks at these areas by asking the questions: How
do they relate to Christ? How does following Christ affect my personal life, my work, my
relationships, and so on?*

Mentoring, *at least when practiced by Christians, certainly ought to center everything on
Christ. But mentoring is less about instruction than it is about initiation—bringing young
men into maturity. Whereas the word "disciple" means "learner," the word protégé
comes from the Latin word meaning "to protect." The mentor's aim is to protect his
young charge as he crosses the frontier into manhood.*

Howard Hendricks, William Hendricks, *As Iron Sharpens Iron: Building Character in a Mentoring Relationship,* ©
1999, Moody Publishers, Chicago, IL. Scripture quotations are taken from the New International Version ("NIV")
Copyright © 1973, 1978, 1984 by International Bible Society.

May 2003

As many of you are aware, I entered Dallas Theological Seminary in 1962 and received my Masters Degree in 1966. During those years I sat under the wonderful teaching of Dr. Howard Hendricks. In the last two years of my study, *'Prof'* invited me and thirteen other men to join him in a weekly study of 1 & 2 Timothy. During that season he encouraged us to focus on Matthew 28:16-20, which our Risen Lord Jesus spoke to His disciples and which *'Prof'* hoped we would incorporate into our life long ministry: ***"All authority has been given to Me in heaven and on earth. Go therefore and make disciples of all the nations, baptizing them in the name of the Father and the Son and the Holy Spirit, teaching them to observe all that I commanded you; and lo, I am with you always, even to the end of the age."*** I have taken that *command* from our Lord and the *challenge* from our *'Prof'* and sought, over the years, to always find the time to disciple men and women in a variety of settings.

I have also learned the wisdom of inviting other brothers to help me disciple young men in what is now called, ***The Timothy Experience.*** For almost a decade now, **Norm Nason,** a Christian businessman and former *Timothy*, has been one of those faithful brothers and together we would like you to meet our current group of disciples.

Brain Berry: I became aware of ***The Timothy Experience*** through Mark Campbell, and the more I heard the more I wanted to get in on the deal. I have been blessed immensely. As the young buck of the group by almost a decade, I'm blessed by the wisdom of life experience that is all around me. I value the chance every Tuesday to interact with and learn from these men as we eat and talk about life and the scriptures. I'm not quite sure what "Tuesday" will hold in the years to follow, but I know that it will be hard to trump the experience I'm living today. What a joy it is to be part of such a dynamic group of men. [**Brian** and **Shannon** have three children and he is an Associate Pastor at *Evangelical Free Church,* in Fremont, CA.]

Mark Campbell: I have been a Christian for some 18 years but I have never been discipled in the manner of Matthew 28:16-20. The experience has been an overwhelming one that has added to my life a sense of unity. I am being taught to study the Word of God seriously, in context, and then apply its truth into my life and ministry. This *Timothy Experience* has been showing me, as a disciple of Jesus, how to be Christ-like in my community, in service to others, in love, truth, confidence and has freed me from the trappings of endless religious programs. The experience has also awakened me to the privilege of becoming part of Christ's great commission in the days ahead. I can't wait to start my first group of disciples and share with them all that I now understand about Christ and His Word. [**Mark** and **Kathleen** have two children and he is a Youth Pastor at *First Baptist Church* in Castro Valley, CA.]

Jim Clansky: I have kind of been appointed the *"man with the newest Bible"* and in many ways this is no doubt a fact! It has been a pleasure to be involved with a group of dedicated Christians where a true atmosphere of family is present. We have had the opportunity to learn about each other's deepest thoughts, problems and blessings and to share our faith as well as learn from one another. The study of Paul's letter to the church at Ephesus has made God's Word clear—we are responsible, by the power of the Holy Spirit, to show our love and concern for others and to reach out to and let others know the value of placing their truth in Jesus as their Savior and Lord. This is a new and exciting step in my life. I personally enjoy the freedom that comes from trusting in Jesus and offering His Word to others. [**Jim**, a Christian businessman, was called into the presence of our Lord and Savior Jesus Christ in September 2005. He is survived by his wife **Jean** who attends *Menlo Park Presbyterian Church* in Menlo Park, CA.]

Don Ott: About a year ago God led me into a mid-life career change, from College Sports to becoming a pastor. While I have been exposed to some of the best training and speakers within the Christian community, I must say that the exposure I've had to biblical discipleship within *The Timothy Experience* has radically changed the course of my life. This is the most significant group I have ever been involved with over the 20+ years of my Christian walk. I began in the group with the mindset that discipleship would be "for me", that I would grow stronger, gain understanding and develop relationships. That did all come true, but at the same time the Holy Spirit etched on my heart that a closer walk and greater knowledge of my Lord Jesus was not just *for me*, but also for others. I am now completely convinced that a lifestyle of intentionally discipling others, as Jesus commanded, pleases Him immensely. I have already begun to train my first group of nine disciples. [**Don** and **Lea** have three children and he is the Associate Pastor of *First Baptist Church of Castro Valley*, CA.]

Chris Pane: I have been a Christian for the past six years and during that time I had read the Bible once. That activity left me thinking that I was well on my way to knowing God and having the wisdom to do something of value with that knowledge. Little did I know, at the time, just how much I needed a discipleship experience within a community of like-minded men who desired to follow the Lord's command as found in Matthew 28:16-20. I also needed to be able to fellowship, pray, and study the Word of God with those same men. Our study is helping us to depend on our Lord and His Holy Spirit for everything in life. We are also learning how to use some of the biblical tools that now bring new life and joy to my personal and group study of the Word of God. I am also looking forward to starting my own discipleship group in the near future. [**Chris** and **Terrie** are both are part of "Marketplace Ministries" and they attend *East Bay Fellowship* in Walnut Creek, CA.]

David Peterson: This time of discipleship has been a wonderful healing experience. At the top of the list would be the love that I have experienced from the leadership and from my fellow disciples. There is an atmosphere of protection, instruction and restoration that permeates our time of fellowship. The value of having a place to ask questions and be honest about your doubts and confusion has been priceless. The time we have spent studying the book of Ephesians has dramatically influenced my relationship to my heavenly Father—I never knew how much I was loved and valued. The truth is finally sinking into my heart and life...*I belong to Jesus!* [**David** is the director of "Men" and "Marketplace Ministries" at *Menlo Park Presbyterian Church* in Menlo Park, CA.]

Mark Rychlik: *The Timothy Experience* is having a profound and eternal impact on my life. First, the foundation of knowledge being provided through books, research papers, the Ephesians study guide, tapes and guest speakers, as well as the teaching guidance which helps us use the tools to draw out spiritual truths independently is so fulfilling. Second, and an equally important catalyst in this life-impact, is the presence of my brothers in Christ. The deep sharing of our lives, watching our growth, and learning to love one another as brothers has helped me to want to choose to fully love others. I'm getting equipped (Ephesians 4:11-13), I'm willing to *just show up* (Ephesians 4:1) and step into the good works God has already prepared for me (Ephesians 2:10). [**Mark** is a Christian businessman and attends *Menlo Park Presbyterian Church* in Menlo Park, CA.]

We have included an invitation form we give to each potential disciple for consideration before they commit to *The Timothy Experience.* This form is given with the hope that it will help some of you to *jump start* your desire to begin your own discipleship group for men or women very soon! Remember, **Matthew 28:16-20** is still a current command in the heart of Christ. (See pages 45-48 for a copy of the Timothy covenant that was sent with this letter.)

Your eternal family because of the *love* of the Lamb of God,   *Ron Anne Marie*

The Timothys

Chris Pane

Norm Nason

Mark Rychlik

Mark Campbell

Ron Ritchie

James Clansky

Don Ott

David Peterson

Brian Berry

Matt. 28:16-20

2 Timothy 2:1-2

In Christ...

Major Ian Thomas

"To be *in Christ* - that is redemption; but for Christ to be *in you* - that is sanctification! To be *in Christ* - that makes you fit for heaven; but for Christ to be *in you* - that makes you fit for earth! To be *in Christ* - that changes your destination; but for Christ to be *in you* - that changes your destiny! The one makes heaven your home - the other makes this world His workshop."

(W. Ian Thomas, *The Saving Life of Christ,*
Zondervan Publishing, © 1972, P. 19)

At the age of twelve he was invited to a Bible study group of the Crusaders' Union by a lad of thirteen who, during that year, received Christ as his Savior. The Bible began to be meaningful to young Ian, and the following summer, still twelve years old, he was converted to Christ at a Crusaders' Union camp. That decision was made when he was alone simply by praying earnestly, "Lord Jesus, please be my Savior"! At the age of fifteen, he felt convinced that he should devote all of his life to the service of the Lord Jesus. He told God that he would become a missionary. He began to preach out in the open air at Hampstead Heath at that early age. He was also actively engaged in Sunday School work as well as in the Crusaders' Bible class. Life became a round of ceaseless activity.

If ever there was any evangelistic activity going on, this youthful zealot was "buzzing around the place, every holiday, every spare moment! Then, one night...I got down on my knees before God, and I just wept in sheer despair. I said, 'Oh, God, I know that I am saved. I love Jesus Christ. I am perfectly convinced that I am converted. With all my heart I have wanted to serve Thee. I have tried to my uttermost and I am a hopeless failure.' That night things happened... God simply focused upon me the Bible message of *Christ Who Is Our Life*. The Lord seemed to make plain to me that night, through my tears of bitterness: 'You see, for seven years, with utmost sincerity, you have been trying to live for Me, on My behalf, the life that I have been waiting for seven years to live through you.'"

That night, all in the space of an hour, Ian Thomas discovered the secret of the adventurous life. He said: "I got up the next morning to an entirely different Christian life, but I want to emphasize this: I had not received one iota more than I had already had for seven years!"

The staff of Peninsula Bible Church took a mission trip to Indonesia in 1984, and during that time we met a young Christian man named **Jimmy Stewart** who was working for an American oil company. When Jimmy came back to the States in 1988, he moved to the Bay Area and attended PBC for a season. The Lord moved Jimmy and his family to Santa Rosa, CA in 1998, where they continue to serve the Lord in their community and church.

Last summer, Jimmy visited me in Menlo Park and asked if I would disciple him. I told him that I was more committed, like Jesus, to spending time with a group of men rather than an individual. He immediately told me that he had a brother with the same heart toward discipleship. We left the meeting excited about the possibility of what God would do in bringing more men together to form a new group. Within a few days he had two more men who were also open to joining our group. As soon as I returned from my vacation, Jimmy called to ask me just how many men he could bring and I told him that my living room would only hold nine. He said that was great because he now had nine men that he would be bringing from the Santa Rosa area.

The men you are going to meet in this letter made a nine month commitment to drive from Santa Rosa to Menlo Park (which is an hour and a half trip, one way) every other Tuesday. Our mornings together would begin at 8:30 AM, in which we would study, have fellowship, pray together and share lunch. After four and a half hours together, they turned around and drove back home. When Jesus said *"All authority has been given to Me in heaven and on earth. Go therefore and make disciples of all the nations, baptizing them in the name of the Father and the Son and the Holy Spirit, teaching them to observe all that I commanded you; and lo, I am with you always, even to the end of the age."* (Matt. 28:16-20), these men took that statement as a *command* rather than a suggestion.

Larry Alford: I decided to join the discipleship group with the hope that one day I would be able to begin my own group. In the beginning of our experience, I was expecting to meet a teacher who would lead us in a structured style and we would listen. However, it soon became apparent that the real leader was the free flowing Spirit of God moving in and through each one of us. I found that approach to study quite refreshing. I now feel more confident that God will use me to help other Christian men that I know to grow in their spiritual walk with Jesus. Another great part of my experience was getting to know other men with very different Christian experiences than my own. It was great to begin to learn who God is, and how to live a life empowered by the Holy Spirit.

Gary Baumbach: As I reflect on my *Timothy Discipleship Experience*, one thing stands out as a primary blessing to me: the discipline of observation in the study of the Word of God. I have now found that my study of the Word and my subsequent teaching of the Word has blossomed to a new level by taking the time to "dig" out the treasures of the original language for myself and then to supplement that study with the many Greek commentaries. The icing on the cake has been to interact with these truths with the wonderful group of brothers that God brought together over these last nine months.

Chris Blaustone: The discipleship experience has been a great time of growth for me as a Christian man. When I was recently considering whether or not I should attend a seminar of an experienced Bible teacher who was coming to our town, an older Christian remarked, "When the giants are in the land drop all you're doing and go see them." I felt the same way when I was invited to become part of this discipleship group. I needed to rearrange my schedule so that I could continue to mature as a disciple of Jesus Christ. This year has proven to be a time of gleaning for me, from men who fervently seek the Lord. Thank you Jesus for being faithful to me!

Pat Craig: Our discipleship experience has been a great leap forward in my personal walk with the Lord Jesus. Learning about real discipleship has forever changed my own ministry. I have learned to investigate the original language of the New Testament, which in turn has dramatically altered the way I preach and teach. I will be forever grateful for the fellowship and friendships that have developed among this group of men – friendships that have led to open doors for ministry and opportunities to extend the Kingdom in an incredibly exciting and fulfilling way.

Bert Hartmann: Each meeting has been filled with fresh joy along with rich teaching and experiential insight. The theme of *Christ living in us* was made so real as we gathered as faithful followers and lovers of Him and each other. I am a choleric temperament fan of using "overwhelming force" but it works so much better when that force is the "overwhelming love" of Christ in us. A good leader is one who is willing to continue to learn from others. What better adventure than to be among brothers growing in the knowledge and application of God's precious Word. I am looking forward to the day when God will use me to lead my own discipleship group and share with them the joy of inductive study of His revelation to us.

Joe Schlabach: As the youngest lion cub of the pride, I have been blessed by our study of the Letter to the Ephesians where we have discovered that *"resurrection power works best in a graveyard."* **(Eph. 2:1-4)** What an awesome God we have, He who has raised us from the dead! What a relief to know that God can do just fine without any of my fleshly efforts to do what only He can do. The Holy Spirit now desires to make the resurrected and invisible Jesus visible in and through me. My "meow" has become His "Roar." Because of the love and grace of God, I am now living a most incredible life.

Greg Sims: I came out of the business world and now my family and I attend a local church where I have the privilege to serve as an Elder. As I look back on the *Timothy Discipleship Experience,* I found myself looking forward to each meeting with great anticipation. I wondered how God was going to use each of us to help one another grow in our spiritual lives. There was always room for the Holy Spirit in the agenda, which made each meeting an adventure. Our inductive work in the Letter to the Ephesians gave me a better understanding of who God is and what He wants to do – in us and through us. My prayer is that we will bring this message back to the people of Sonoma County. I am also praying that they will truly feel the presence of Jesus in our lives and we would allow Him to reach out, through us, to touch them with His love.

Jimmy Stewart: I realize how blessed I have been in getting to observe and experience authentic Biblical discipleship. Using the Ephesians Letter by the Apostle Paul, we discovered our Relationship with God the Father, Son and Holy Spirit (*The New Covenant*), as well as our Relationship with the Body of Christ, and the world *(Body Life)* and the Relationship with the Enemy *(Spiritual Warfare)*. These are the truths that I want to use to help men and women understand the essentials of their relationship with God, their fellow man, and the enemy, who seeks like a lion to destroy the very relationships we hold so dearly. I have also learned you cannot put LIFE into a bottle.

Randy Watson: As a former missionary and church planting pastor, I have found our discipleship experience to be a *real* experience. I have been renewed in my commitment to know the Truth and to preach the Truth with clarity and power.

We have included the invitation form that we give each new potential disciple to look over before they make a commitment to the Lord Jesus and to the *Timothy Discipleship Experience.* We share this form with you with the hope that it will help some of you to "jump-start" your desire to begin your own discipleship group. Matthew 28:16-20 is still a current **command** in the heart of Jesus.

Your eternal family because of the love of the Father and his Beloved Lamb,   *Ron Anne Marie*

2003/04 Timothys

Back row: **Ron, Randy, Larry, Jim, Greg and Chris**
Front row: **Pat, Joe, Gary and Bert**

Lessons Learned
A Timothy Exerience

I believe it's no coincidence that part of our Timothy experience has had to do with a truck and a van as object lesson in God's greater plan; for the lives of this group of men, things we need to learn again and again.

Lesson one: it's not always about the destination but what you learn working through the frustration of event, not going by the set time table, as God shows us, again, that He is able to take heated engines or gas mixed with diesel and paint something beautiful on His awesome easel—a canvas that explodes with the beauty of His grace shining through the hearts and into the faces of this band of men. I have come to love operating in His Spirit, powered from above. Whether laying hands and praying on my van's hood, or Greg and Jim believing what they really should have, that in fact Bert is not totally perfect and did fall into the sin of Chevron fueling neglect. Lesson one reminds us that it's not about us, but about Him as the pressures of life cut and polish a gem that reflects the light of His life in and through us; an on-going process we love to discuss.

Lesson two: it's not always about the destination but what you learn through driving conversations. Early morning wisdom is what we yearn for, look out guys we missed the Sandhill turn! Sharing our lives, fears, doubts and dreams as the Spirit shapes a Tuesday driving theme. Reviewing Greek or reflecting on Wuest, preparing for our Tuesday morning feast. The driving conversation sets the breakfast table so when we reach Reminder Ron's, we are able and ready for a Timothy experience that is sweet; provided that each of us remembers to wipe his feet.

Lesson three: sometimes *it is* about the destination, especially if you've taken the time in study and preparation. If not, time was limited, a little bit of a con. You can count on the words, "You'll be riding with Ron." How deep our conversations and sharing, as the Spirit moved us into caring about the teaching moment at hand, even when it did not fit the lesson plan. At moments, for some, a little scary but God is good, and we finished Ephesians, Larry!

Lesson four: sometimes it's about the destination as God opens new doors of revelation. The Holy Spirit enters His key into our hearts and unlocks a mystery. Whether it's Ron's heart for his Anne Marie displayed for all of us to see as he ministered to us dead tired while she's hospitalized; weary and wired. Or my pains and hurts laid bear as Randy taught and we were all able to share in the moment as the Spirit moved us to care for each other; a very transparent loving day. Why on earth would we want to live any other way!

Lesson five, is true of all of us; we are all bozo's on this bus! Clowns, idiots, jesters and fools ransomed, redeemed, now given the tools to help other beggars find the Bread of Heaven that feeds soul, spirit and head. A company of pastors and wannabes learning to live life open and free from the shackles of convention and staid form, not being molded by tradition or the norm; Oh, my the church just left the building to this concept we bozos are ever yielding. Ministering clowns in the circus tent of life, living new covenant lives through joy and strife; reaching a body that sometimes doesn't know it needs a hand committed to the His work in us is where we stand. This is the heartfelt essence of lesson five, towards which this group of Timothys continues to strive.

Lesson six: there can be a level of frustration as we place into the body—for their consideration—principles of discipleship and dynamic life, much of which cuts deep like the surgeon's knife and bloody cries come as healing is done, as the body has surgery performed by the Son. His Body, His cutting, His healing, we remain faithful to His truth; unyielding. Run the race and seek the prize, not growing weary; no room for compromise.

Lesson seven: a disciple's life is never boring! Deep in the trenches or on mountain tops soaring, the life of Christ, fully functional in you and me, His life reflected for all the world to see. As Reminder Ron has taught me to say, "Why would I want to live any other way!"

Poetically submitted for your consideration by your fellow Timothy in Christ, Gary July, 2004

We were just getting over the joy of the Christmas holidays, which were filled with family and friends, when my accountant reminded me of a January 15th tax deadline. My February calendar reminded me to prepare to celebrate Groundhog Day on the 2nd, Abe Lincoln's birthday on the 12th, followed quickly by Valentine's Day on the 14th and then Washington's birthday on 22nd. We may have to look for a night job to cover all the expenses! The world has a way of trying to keep our attention away from keeping the main thing *the right thing*. And one of *the right things* in our lives is to keep our focus on the Lord Jesus Christ, and honoring him by participating in all that he asks us to be and do during our short stay on this earth.

One of *the right things* our Lord Jesus has encouraged all of us to do is to remain faithful to the ministry of discipleship. At this time, I am involved with six former disciples, all who have committed themselves to disciple 15 new disciples over a period of 12-16 months. Our motivation comes from the lips of our risen Lord Jesus when he appeared to his eleven disciples in Galilee, just before he returned to heaven. He reminded them that: ***"…All authority has been given to Me in heaven and on earth. Go therefore and make disciples of all the nations, baptizing them in the name of the Father and the Son and the Holy Spirit, teaching them to observe all that I commanded you; and lo, I am with you always, even to the end of the age."*** (Matthew 28:16-20, NASB.)

Dallas Willard wrote; *"As a disciple of Jesus I am with him by choice and by grace, learning from him how to live in the Kingdom of God…his life flowing through mine…. I am learning from Jesus to live my life as he would live my life if he were I. I am not necessarily learning to do everything he did, but I am learning how to do every thing I do in the manner that he did all that he did."* (**The Divine Conspiracy**, p. 283.)

John R.W. Stott wrote: *"The numbers of people coming to Christ around the world are staggering. Today we are witnessing perhaps one of the greatest expansions of the Church worldwide, especially in the Two-Thirds World. These numbers would suggest great success stories—the mission of the Church is being accomplished. And yet, very reputable and deeply committed church leaders from Two-Thirds World countries are quick to note that the Church is exploding with extraordinary numerical growth without depth. We are witnessing one of the most **over-evangelized**, but **under-discipled** eras in history."* (**M. Sawyer - In the Gap**, John Stott Ministries, p. 1, 12/02.)

Howard and William Hendricks wrote: *"…Discipleship involves a call, a direct invitation from the teacher that borders on a command…The word **disciple** means "learner." In Jesus' day, teachers roamed the ancient world recruiting bands of "learners" who then followed these masters and adopted their teaching. Sometimes the disciples became masters themselves and developed their own followings. But Jesus' command to His followers to **"go and make disciples of all nations"** (Matthew 28:16-20) is distinctive in that Jesus remains the Master, the Discipler. He wants people who are recruited to the faith to remain His disciples, His learners. Discipleship, as we know it today, tends to narrow its focus to the spiritual dimension. Ideally, it should touch every area of life—our personal life and lifestyle, our work, our relationships."* (**Iron Sharpens Iron**, Moody Press, 1995. P. 182-183.)

Please keep us in your prayers as we seek to be faithful to our Risen Lord Jesus in keeping the main thing *the right thing* with his command to ***"Go and make disciples."*** Thank you for all your prayers and support on our behalf.

Your eternal family because of the *love* of the Father and His beloved Lamb,   *Ron Anne Marie*

My "Timothy" experience

by RJ Ritchie

This photo was taken in March, 2007 at the door of the "Empty Tomb" located outside the walls of Jerusalem, which is where Ron Sr. declared Jesus as his resurrected Lord and Savior in 1955.

The Timothy Discipleship Experience was valuable in fulfilling my desire to learn about the life of Jesus to better understand what it means to become his true disciple, and to learn how to study the Word of God to gain a better understanding of who God is and why He wants a relationship with all of us.

Twelve of us met every Tuesday night for 18 months, learning how to study the Bible inductively and learning how to prepare an overview of the text with the goal of teaching our study to the class. Together we read and discussed the content of books by authors such as Dietrich Bonhoeffer and James Montgomery Boice, writers who challenged the way we think about God the Father, His Son, and the Holy Spirit. But for me, the most rewarding part of the experience was the time spent praying for one another and growing together with a common goal: to proclaim the "good news" of Jesus Christ to our world in our generation.

The Timothy Discipleship Experience offered both hard work and new spiritual challenges, but the reward was far greater than the sacrifice. I came away from the "Timothys" having more confidence in who my God is and who I am as a man in Christ.

"How rich is a man who loves our Lord and loves others, making disciples along the way!" - RJ Ritchie

Pass The Torch!

We are reminded by the apostle Paul in 2 Timothy 2:1-10 of the value and need to continue to *pass the torch* of the *sacred deposit of truth—the truth of salvation—*given to us by our risen Lord Jesus through his faithful disciples in every generation up to this very moment. Paul wanted Timothy and all future generations of disciples to:

1. Remember the Faithfulness of Past Generations   2:1-2
2. Remain Faithful to Jesus   2:3-7
3. Remember We Serve a Living Savior   2:8-10

1.   Remember the Faithfulness of Past Generations (2 Timothy 2:1-2)

"You then, my son, be strong in the grace that is in Christ Jesus. And the things you have heard me say in the presence of many witnesses entrust to reliable men [and women] **who will also be qualified to teach others."**

a.   **The Past:** The aged apostle Paul, citizen of Rome and citizen of heaven, was between a rock and a hard place in 66 AD. In between the years 57-59 AD, Paul left Ephesus in Turkey with plans to visit the Christians in Jerusalem. During his visit to the Temple, some Jewish Zealots from Asia saw him and began loudly accusing him, "This is the man who preaches to all men everywhere against our people, and the Law, and this place and besides he has even brought Greeks into the temple and has defiled this holy place" (Acts 21:28). The apostle would have been killed had it not been for the Roman cohort who had taken him by night to their seaside garrison in Caesarea where, for the next two years, he awaited trial on the trumped up charges made by those Jewish Zealots. Finally, Paul took advantage of his Roman citizenship and "appealed to Caesar" and was shipped to Rome to await trial. He was placed under house arrest for the next two years.

It appears that he was *set free* in 63 AD. He traveled to the island of <u>Crete</u> with his disciple and *"true son,"* Titus, and left him there to *"straighten out what was left unfinished and appoint elders in every town"* (Titus 1:5). The apostle then went to the port city of <u>Ephesus</u> and visited the church there with his other *"true son in the faith,"* Timothy (1 Timothy 1:2), *"to command certain men not to teach false doctrine"* as well as *"set in place godly elders"* (1 Timothy 3). Paul then went on to northern Greece where he wrote the letters we now call 1 Timothy and Titus. However, sometime in 66 AD, between his visits to Corinth and Rome, he was arrested once again and taken to the royal city of Rome. As he became a prisoner of Jesus Christ for *preaching* the gracious Good News of his Lord and Savior, Nero, the Roman Emperor, was *preaching* the elimination of Christianity. Paul was placed in a cold and damp underground dungeon and chained to the wall (Ray Stedman and I visited that dungeon on his birthday in October, 1972). As he sat in that dungeon, Paul wrote to Timothy: "At my first defense, no one came to my support, but everyone deserted me…except our risen Lord who stood beside me and gave me strength." During that arrest, only his faithful friend Dr. Luke remained at his side (2 Timothy 4:9-18).

b.   **The Present:** The aged apostle knew his time on earth was coming to an end, and he wanted to let Timothy know his spiritual state: "For I am already being poured out like a drink offering, and the time has come for my departure" (2 Timothy 4:6).

c.   **The Future:** Paul was not only conscious of the **past** and the present but he was also conscious of all the possible *future generations* to come and he wanted the Good News of Jesus Christ to be offered to them so they could also enjoy the pleasures of eternal life now, and into the life to come. So perhaps, in his mind's eye, he visualized that as the Greeks had used *torchbearers* to announce the forthcoming Olympic Games throughout the Roman Empire, so he had been chosen by God to become one of His *torchbearers*, for he had been holding up the light and truth of Jesus Christ as he ran for some 33 years throughout the Roman, Greek and Jewish villages announcing the Good News. At the same time, as he sat in his cold and damp dungeon, he must of realized that it was time to **"pass that torch"** to his younger son Timothy with the hope that those future generations would not only hear, but accept the gift of eternal life that could only be found in His Lord and Savior Jesus Christ. As he prepared to **"pass the torch"** to Timothy, he wrote with mixed metaphors: "I have fought the good fight, I have finished the race, and I have kept the faith. Now there is in store for me the crown of righteousness, which the Lord, the righteous Judge, will award to me on that day – and not only to me, but also to all who have longed for his appearing" (2 Timothy 4:7-8).

d. **Spiritual Relationship:** *"You then my son..."* Timothy, (which in Greek means "God-honoring one") was a young man whom Paul had meet in Lystra, Turkey, during his first missionary journey (47-48 AD, see Acts 16:1-5). Timothy's unbelieving father was Greek, but he had heard about the coming Messiah from the teaching of his godly Jewish mother and grandmother. When Paul visited his home town of Lystra and preached the Good News of Jesus Christ, Timothy listened and in time bowed his heart to Jesus as Lord (1 Corinthians 4:17) and they ministered together over the next 15 years. Paul had already written to Timothy in his first letter on how, as a young man, he should conduct his ministry in Ephesus. In that letter, he addressed him as "My true Son in the faith…" (1 Timothy 1:2) and he wanted to remind him "Don't let anyone look down on you because you are young, but set an example for the believers in speech, in life, in love, in faith and in purity" (1 Timothy 4:12). In this letter, he addressed him as "My dear son…" encouraging him to "Do your best to present yourself to God as one approved, a workman who does not need to be ashamed and who correctly handles the word of truth" (2 Timothy 2:15). One can gather from these statements the reality of a relationship in which a loving, gracious and faithful Father was seeking to guide his deeply appreciative, humble son.

e. **Strength out of weakness:** *"...My son be strong in the grace that is in Christ Jesus."* Timothy had an emotional makeup which would not impress anyone as one of the up and coming new leaders of the growing church of Ephesus. In reality, at the time of Paul's final imprisonment Timothy was a young man in his mid-thirties, with some physical illnesses that kept him physically weak. At the same time, he had emotional struggles that kept him timid and withdrawn, causing him to be a follower rather than a leader. But Paul was not counting on Timothy to rely on his own strength to accomplish his ministry. That physical, emotional and spiritual strength would be provided by the love and grace of our risen Lord and Savior Jesus Christ who lived within him. Paul understood that spiritual reality very clearly when he wrote to the Corinthians about how he had asked he Lord to remove his "thorn in the flesh." The Lord responded that He would not remove that thorn for Paul needed to learn: "My grace is sufficient for you, for power is perfected in weakness. Most gladly, therefore, I will rather boast of my weaknesses, that the power of Christ may dwell in me" (2 Corinthians 12:7-10).

f. **Take in the truth:** *"And the things you have heard me say in the presence of many witnesses."* Paul then had Timothy think back over their last 15 years of ministry together, which took place primarily within their second and third missionary journeys. He reminded Timothy what he wrote to the Philippians in Greece after their visit with them concerning the Person of Jesus Christ: **1)** *"For to me to live is Christ and to die is gain..."* (1:21); **2)** *"Have this attitude in yourselves which was also in Christ Jesus...taking the form of a bondservant..."* (2:7); **3)** *"That I may know Him and the power of His resurrection and the fellowship of His suffering being conformed to his death..."* (3:10); and, **4)** *"I can do all things through Him who strengthens me"* (4:13). He reminded Timothy of the time when he sought to reason with the Jews in Thessalonica, Greece from the Scriptures, "explaining and giving evidence that Christ had to suffer and rise again from the dead" and saying, "This Jesus whom I am proclaiming to you is the Christ" (Acts 17:2-3). And, of the time in Ephesus, where over a period of two years he sought to reason daily in the school of Tyrannus about the whole council of God (Acts 19:9-10; 21:27).

g. **Share the gold:** *"...Entrust* [to deposit as a trust] *to reliable* [trustworthy] *men* [and women] *who will also be qualified to teach others...."* There were many unreliable men in Paul's experience who had heard the Good News of Jesus Christ and yet had deserted both the faith and the apostle. Men like, "…Demas having loved this present world, and Alexander the coppersmith did me much harm." At the same time, there remained the reliable men and women like Dr. Luke and Titus, and the godly couple named Aquila and Priscilla just to name but a few (2 Timothy 4). Paul had received the deposit of truth of Jesus Christ by a revelation of God beginning with his experience with the risen and now living Lord Jesus on the Damascus Road (Acts 9; Galatians 1:11-12). Then, at the end of his life and ministry, Paul said to Timothy "Don't be ashamed of the testimony of our Lord...but join with me in the suffering for the gospel according to the power of God, who has saved us, and called us with a holy calling, not according to our works, but according to His own purpose and grace which was granted us in Christ Jesus for all eternity, but now has been revealed by the appearing of our Savior Christ Jesus, who abolished death, and brought life and immortality to light through the gospel...For this reason I also suffer these things, but I am not ashamed, for I know whom I have believed and I am convinced that He is able to guard what I have entrusted to Him until that day." (2 Timothy 1:8-12.)

We can then imagine Paul saying to his spiritual son: "Well Timothy, having taken in all this spiritual truth which I received from our Lord, concerning the love and grace of God, I am now going to give it to you. I want to encourage you to share it with reliable men and women who will then, in their time, be able to teach the truth of Jesus Christ and His gift of salvation to the future generations of reliable men and women until He returns." (See Matthew 28:16-20).

Spiritual Principle: The Old Testament believers always thought about life and the truth of God in terms of past, present and future generations. They understood, beginning with Abraham, that God's history of salvation was bigger than their own generation. (Refer to Genesis 12-15; Psalm 78.)

Illustration: In the summer of 1969, while I was a youth pastor at the Walnut Creek Presbyterian Church, Dave Roper, who was the youth pastor at Peninsula Bible Church in Palo Alto, CA (across the San Francisco bay) and I decided to bring our two groups together at the Ponderosa Lodge in Mount Hermon, CA (I was finishing my ministry at Walnut Creek and had planned to begin my new ministry at PBC in September of that year). That started the first of many Student Discipleship weeks. There were some 200 students in attendance at that first conference. Ponderosa Lodge had provided for us a young and very talented musician (a recent graduate from Wheaton College) named John Fischer. John's plans were to work that summer at the lodge and then go on to seminary in the fall. We had a wonderful week of music and teaching together and the Lord showed us that we all had kinder spirits for the Lord and His ministry.

At the end of that week, I spent some time with John talking over his future. He really wanted to grow in his relationship and knowledge of the Lord, but he wasn't so sure he should go to seminary. As soon as I got home, I called Dave Roper, told him of our talk, and told him that I had asked John to wait for a call from us before he made any decision about the future. Dave said, "Why don't you ask him to become a PBC Intern?" I was so excited by the possibility that I called John right away and offered him the opportunity to come and serve the Lord with us at PBC in the fall. I will always remember John asking me, "What is an Intern?" I stumbled over my answer and asked him to trust God to open the door for him to come and serve with us for the next two years.

John came and served the Lord faithfully for more than two years, married a godly woman named Marty, and then the Lord blessed them with three children. He produced many musical records and CD's, and has become known nationally and internationally as a fine musician, teacher and author of some 15 books. John, to me, is but one of the many wonderful stories of men and women who chose to take the time to be discipled by faithful men and women (in the past) and who is now discipling men and women in their generation.

The disciples of Jesus Christ were (and presently are) called to remember how the faithful followers of Jesus Christ in their generation *passed the torch of truth* to our generation. And to remember that we are called upon to pass that same torch of truth to reliable men and women of the next generations who will be able to teach others in each future generation until Christ returns to set up His kingdom on earth.

## 2.	Remain Faithful to Jesus (2 Timothy 2:3-7)

"Endure hardship with us like a good soldier of Christ Jesus. No one serving as a <u>soldier</u> gets involved in civilian affairs—he wants to please his commanding officer. Similarly, if anyone competes as an <u>athlete</u>, he does not receive the victor's crown unless he competes according to the rules. The hardworking <u>farmer</u> should be the first to receive a share of the crops. Reflect on what I am saying, for the Lord will give you insight into all this."

Paul used *three metaphors* out of the daily life of the Roman, Greek and Jewish cultures to encourage the *timid* Timothy and the Christians in Ephesus, as well as future generations, to remain faithful to our Lord Jesus Christ in the political, social and Christian communities until He comes again.

a.	**Good Solider:** *"Endure hardship with us like a good soldier of Christ Jesus. No one serving as a soldier gets involved in civilian affairs – he wants to please his commanding officer..."* There are <u>three</u> <u>key</u> <u>phrases</u> in this verse: *Endure hardship, avoid entanglement* in the many world arenas, and *develop a heart to please your Lord.* Paul, as a Roman citizen, and at times a Roman prisoner, had more than enough opportunities to observe, as well as hear and speak to Roman soldiers. **1)** *Endure hardship*: In time he learned that they had to endure lots of hardship, especially in times of war or civil unrest within certain cities like Rome and Jerusalem. As a loyal Roman soldier, Paul understood that built into his time of service were times of hardship. In the same manner the loyal Christian who is engaged in the daily battle with the world, the flesh, and the devil, he too must suffer hardships. **2)** *Avoid entanglement*: No soldier can serve two masters; he must choose to either serve his commanding officer to achieve certain military objectives, or some Roman politician and his personal or civil ambitions. Paul would later remind Timothy that, *"...Demas, because he loved this world, has deserted me and gone to Thessalonica"* (2 Timothy 4:9). **3)** *Develop a heart to please your Lord*: Paul encouraged Timothy: "...Flee the evil desires of youth, and pursue righteousness, faith, love, and peace...out of a pure heart" (2:22).

b.	**A Good Athlete:** *"...if anyone competes as an athlete, he does not receive the victor's crown unless he competes according to the rules."* Paul was very familiar with the spirit of competition exhibited in the Greek Games. He was also familiar with what the athletes understood in their day, as we understand in our sports world today, that they received no crown unless they competed according to the rules. In other words: "no rules, no wreath." Paul had ministered over the past 33 years within the moral rules of God, which were placed in his heart as part of the terms of the *New Covenant*. He had sought as a lifestyle to depend on the indwelling power of the Holy Spirit to faithfully run the race with spiritual integrity. Paul reminded Timothy that, "...I have finished the course...in the future there is laid up for me the crown of righteousness...which the righteous Judge will award to me on that day...and to all who love his appearing" (4:7-8).

c.	**A Good Farmer:** *"The hardworking farmer should be the first to receive a share of the crops."* Paul offered <u>two</u> <u>key ideas</u>: *hard work*, and the joy of being one of *the first to receive a share of the crop.* I plowed many a field as a youth on a farm of some 300 acres. From experience I know that you not only have to plow the field, but you then have to go over it a second time with a tiller, and then you have to go over it a third time to spread manure and chemicals to keep it enriched and to protect the soil from deadly insects. Only then do you spend days planting the new seed, watering the fields, and when the first stalks come up you need to go over the whole field again and cultivate it so the weeds won't choke the new crop. Then, you wait for good weather, walk the fields checking the crops and looking for the proper moment to begin the harvest. Finally, after weeks and months of waiting, depending on the crops you have planted, you get the word "harvest time" and you join a whole crew of men and women who go into the fields working night and day until it is all harvested. It is only after the harvest time is finished that you get the delightful opportunity to share in the **first fruits of your hard work**. "Do not be deceived: God cannot be mocked. A man reaps what he sows. The one who sows to please his sinful nature, from that nature will reap destruction; the one who sows to please the Spirit, from the Spirit will reap eternal *life*. Let us not become weary in doing good, for at the proper time we will reap a harvest if we do not give up" (Galatians 6:7-9).

Spiritual Principle: Paul used three metaphors to help us remember the faithfulness of Jesus. In verse 4:13, Paul quoted a trustworthy source saying: *"If we are faithless, He will remain faithful, for He cannot disown himself."* As the focused soldier, the competing athlete, and the hardworking farmer remained faithful to their calling, so we are to be faithful to our calling to **"pass the torch"** of spiritual truth received from Jesus Christ to the next generation of trustworthy men and women who will, in time, then pass it on to future generations until He comes again. *"Reflect on what I am saying, for the Lord will give you insight into all this."*

Illustration: One day Steve Zeisler (who is currently a pastor at PBC and a disciple of Dave Roper) asked me if I would consider working with a young Intern named Jeff Farrar. Steve had been discipling him for a year and he thought that Jeff might benefit by joining our team of Interns working with our "Careers Alive" singles ministry. I arranged an interview with Jeff, who turned out to be a delightful young man. I told him that I might be interested in having him join us, but I would need to call around and get some feedback on his study and work habits. During those phone calls, I discovered that Jeff had some weaknesses that would harm our team and ministry at that time so I sent him a letter of regret. A week later he came up to the door of my office, stuck his head inside and said, "I got your letter. I showed it to

my father and he told me that he had been trying to tell me the same things for several years. I then took your letter to my Bible study group and read it to them and they agree with its content. So I wonder if you would reconsider taking me on as part of your team so that I could be challenged and grow out of those areas of weakness." I said, "Jeff, any man who has the courage to come back to me after receiving that kind of letter is already on the team! Welcome to a great new adventure." Jeff went on to become a wonderful pastor among the flock of Central Peninsula Church in Foster City, California, as well as a national and international preacher, teacher and discipler. He also created a well-known ministry called "Higher Power" which was designed to help men and women struggling with a variety of chemical addictions. Jeff eventually had to leave full-time ministry because of physical problems, but his disciples are faithfully ***passing the torch of spiritual truth*** on to this generation.

We are called upon to **remember the faithfulness of the past generations** who ***passed the torch of spiritual truth*** to reliable men and women in our generation, and then we are to **remain faithful to our Lord Jesus as we *pass the torch of spiritual truth*** to reliable men and women in the very next generation until He comes again in power and glory. **The key that will help us *remain faithful* is to remember that we serve a living Savior.**

3. Remember We Serve A Living Savior (2 Timothy 2:8-10)

"Remember Jesus Christ, raised from the dead, descended from David. This is my gospel, for which I am suffering even to the point of being chained like a criminal. But God's word is not chained. Therefore, I endure everything for the sake of the elect, that they too may obtain the salvation that is in Christ Jesus, with eternal glory."

a. **Remember our Living Hope:** *"Remember Jesus Christ, raised from the dead, descended from David. This is my gospel..."* Jesus was the ideal suffering soldier, athlete and farmer, and because of His death, burial and resurrection, He is now being crowned with glory and honor. The incarnation and resurrection of the Son of Man, Son of God, were the two truths denied by the heretics, but the very truths that kept Paul faithful in the midst of his suffering. Jesus, who suffered, has not only been raised from the dead by his Father, but is still alive and among us and in us forever. Jesus is now our Savior and King. The apostle had stated that truth so well to the Corinthians: "Now, brothers, I want to remind you of the gospel I preached to you, which you received and on which you have taken your stand. By this gospel you are saved, if you hold firmly to the word I preached to you. Otherwise, you have believed in vain. For what I received I passed on to you as of first importance: that Christ died for our sins according to the Scriptures, that he was buried, that he was raised on the third day according to the Scriptures..." (1 Corinthians 15:1-4). The apostle Peter wrote to the Asian Christians in 62 AD: "Praise be to the God and Father of our Lord Jesus Christ! In his great mercy he has given us new birth into a living hope through the resurrection of Jesus Christ from the dead..." (1 Peter 1:3). Paul's basic point to Timothy was that as Christ suffered in the flesh in order to give us the joy of eternal life, so will we at times suffer as we seek *to pass the torch of the His Good News* in a fallen and broken world; first the cross, and then the crown.

b. **Remember as Christ suffered so we are called to suffer:** *"...for which I am suffering even to the point of being chained like a criminal. But God's word is not chained..."* Paul was chained as an innocent Roman citizen in the same manner that our innocent Lord Jesus was imprisoned and suffered under Rome in Jerusalem some 30 years earlier. After His death, burial and resurrection, Jesus met Paul on the Damascus Road in the midst of his persecution of Christ's followers. He was taken blind to the house of a faithful disciple named Judas. Jesus then told Ananias, another disciple living in the same town, to visit Paul and lay his hands on him so he would receive his sight once again. Ananias was fearful because of Saul's past evil reputation. But the Risen Lord said to him: "Go for he is a chosen vessel of Mine, to bear My name before the Gentiles, and kings, and the children of Israel, for I will show him how much he must suffer for My name sake" (Acts 9:10-16). As seen so many times in the book of Acts, you can chain the messenger but not the word of God. So Timothy…**when you are tempted to avoid pain, humiliation, suffering or death in your ministry remember Jesus Christ and think again."** (John R.W. Stott, *Guard the Gospel*, p. 62)

c. **The main thing must remain the *right* Person:** *"Therefore, I endure everything for the sake of the elect that they too may obtain the salvation that is in Christ Jesus, with eternal glory."* Paul was very conscious that his present imprisonment with all of its physical, emotional and spiritual sufferings had something to do with the salvation of the chosen ones of God. He went about the Roman Empire preaching the Good News of Jesus Christ: "Everyone who calls on the name of the Lord will be saved. How, then, can they call on the one they have not believed in? And how can they believe in the one of whom they have not heard? And how can they hear without someone preaching to them? And how can they preach unless they are sent? As it is written, How beautiful are the feet of those who bring good news!" (Romans 10:13-15). Because the Good News was in such contrast to the current lifestyles of the Roman, Greek, Jewish and Barbarian societies, it caused most of them to react in fear and strike out at the message and the messenger.

Spiritual Principles: May Paul's last words become ours: "I have fought the good fight, I have finished the course, I have kept the faith; in the future there is laid up for me, the crown of righteousness, which the Lord, the righteous Judge, will award to me on that day, and not only to me, but also to all who have loved His appearing." (2 Timothy 4:7-8.)

Illustration: A few months before Ray C. Stedman, formerly our faithful pastor at Peninsula Bible Church in Palo Alto for some 40 years, would be carried by angels into the presence of His beloved Lord Jesus (Oct. 1992), he came down to Palo Alto from his home in Oregon. The word went out to both the North (PBC in Palo Alto) and South (PBC Cupertino) elders and pastors that he would like to meet with all of us. We gathered together in a large circle in the Fireside room at PBC North, knowing that Ray's days were numbered on this earth. Ray, this great friend, pastor, teacher, discipler and spiritual brother to so many, looked around the room that was filled with people that he poured his life into over the years, people that he had equipped to *"pass the torch"* of the Good News of Jesus Christ into the present and future generations. He began the meeting by picking out several people and reminding them of some great trips they took together overseas, or some wonderful campus ministry they had together, as well as the many wonderful times they had had while preaching and teaching at PBC. We all laughed and cried together that night. Then, he finished the evening by reminding all of us who were now the shepherds of the flock of God to keep the main thing the main Person: *"The Good News of the gospel of Jesus Christ, the freeing truths of the New Covenant and the need to continue to love one another."* We then prayed together with hearts filled with love, truth, joy, and sorrow.

When the meeting was over, Ray stood up and each person, in turn, hugged him with hearts filled with loving tenderness and thankfulness for his life, love and faithfulness to his Lord and Savior Jesus Christ and to all of us. That whole memorial evening I felt like one of the Ephesian elders who came down to met Paul at the docks of Miletus, Turkey on his way to Jerusalem. At that meeting they heard him say, "You know how I lived the whole time I was with you, from the first day I came into the province of Asia (or Palo Alto, in this case). I served the Lord with great humility and with tears…You know that I have not hesitated to preach anything that would be helpful to you but have taught you publicly and from house to house. I have declared to both Jews and Greeks that they must turn to God in repentance and have faith in our Lord Jesus…However, I consider my life worth nothing to me, if only I may finish the race and complete the task the Lord Jesus has given me…the task of testifying to the gospel of God's grace. When he had said this, he knelt down with all of them and prayed. They all wept as they embraced him and kissed him. What grieved them most was his statement that they would never see his face again" (Acts 20:17-38).

In summary, we are called upon to remember the faithfulness of the past generations and to remain faithful to the Lord Jesus. It was He who *passed the torch of spiritual truth* to Paul, who passed it to Timothy, who passed it on to reliable men and women, who were able to teach others the same eternal truth. And, in time, they passed it on to our generation with the hope that we will remain faithful to our Lord in continuing to *pass the torch* on to the next generation until He comes again in power and glory.

The key that will help us remain faithful is to *remember we serve a risen Savior* and He is in our hearts today!

His name is Jesus!

PRAYER OR SOMETHING.....

by Brian C Berry

Only once in my life has anyone ever confronted me on my prayer life.

No, not like if I pray or when do I pray, but actually on how I pray. It came from Ron Ritchie, a trusted 70 year old mentor. I was 32ish when he looked me in the eye over lunch and in a way only a man who looks like Moses/Grizzly Adams could have said, "Brian, you use God's name like a comma when you pray. God I pray that (comma God) you would help me do blah blah blah (comma God).... "I think it was the first time in my life I'd actually truly thought about how I spoke to God and what words I chose.

He also introduced me for the first time to the ***PRAYER TOAST***. We did it every night after bible study with Ron and our clan of disciples over dinner for a year of Tuesday's. I use it all the time in restaurants now. Rather than bowing your head and wondering if you're going to get the prayer done before the waiter returns to interrupt you awkwardly, you just ditch the head bowed deal, grab your beverage, raise it to the sky, and thank Jesus for the fellowship, the food you're about to eat, the amazing chance to enjoy breath in your lungs, and invite God's presence to be at the table with you. It's really refreshing. You should try it sometime. Inviting God to join your table and thanking him for the blessings of food and friends is always sincere and very rare today.

Well anyway, ever since that year of prayer challenges by Ron, I've been particularly sensitive to my own prayers and annoyed by some of the traditional habits of the church today in prayer. A couple of things that have happened this week made me think of it, so I decided to blog them. Here you go, here's my list:

- ***THE ANNOUNCEMENT PRAYER:*** This is not really a prayer at all. It's not really talking to God; it's just talking to people while they are in the hypnotic state of eyes closed and heads bowed. It often involves transition hints like, "as the band comes up" or reminders like, "we know that this week is the big blah blah blah".
- ***THE HOUDINI PRAYER:*** This may or may not be sincere prayer, but it is strategically placed so that we magically whip people on and off stage while your eyes are closed. While you're supposedly talking to God, the band can magically disappear and the speaker appears or vice versa- as if the angel of the Lord himself whisked them off the stage like Houdini.
- ***THE NO ONE'S LOOKING PRAYER:*** This is the prayer where we begin by talking to God, then pause to talk to you, asking no one to look around, cuz evidently that screws up the sincerity of someone really talking to God. Now, while "no one's looking, please raise your hand or look at me or whatever..." cuz now we're pausing in prayer to talk to you all.
- ***THE GOD IS A COMMA/MUST LOVE TO HEAR HIS OWN NAME PRAYER:*** This prayer is one I was very good at and have tried to ditch. It's the prayer that uses God more times in one sentence than is humanly possible. It is common, but evidently only something we do in prayer. Can you imagine saying to me at dinner, "Dear Brian, thanks so much Brian for having us over for dinner Brian. I just love you Brian. Brian you have blessed us so much Brian that we wanted to tell you Brian that we are here to serve you Brian with our whole lives Brian. Amen Brian. Amen." Yeah, it sounds stupid, but if you insert God in there for me, well, you have the classic comma/name prayer.
- ***THE END THE MEETING PRAYER:*** This prayer is just a prayer we do cuz the meeting is over and evidently, no two Christians are allowed to talk and then leave without praying to sorta close the book on this deal. Most of the world just says, see you later. Christians feel the need to make sure God knows we're done talking now.
- ***THE IN CASE GOD WASN'T LISTENING PRAYER:*** This is where we go around the room and have everyone share prayer requests. Then, after we have talked to one another for a while about them, we then repeat exactly what we've all been talking about but now, we do it with sentences that begin with "Dear God" and end with "Amen" since evidently when we were saying them before, we were talking to ourselves and God was busy somewhere else.
- ***THE GOSSIP PRAYER:*** This is a classic one. This often never makes it to prayer. But under the umbrella of protection of a prayer request, we gossip about others so that the person who is receiving the juicy facts can take them back and pray about them.
- ***THE SUPER SPIRITUAL PRAYER:*** This one is where the person praying uses words that only God can understand and that are only used when praying. It's often with hands held up, sounds really super theological, and usually gets them asked to pray a lot, cuz it sounds like something God himself might say in 1850.
- ***THE IT'S TIME TO SHUT UP PRAYER:*** This prayer is not really prayer. It's just a reality that the one at the mic is being ignored, so instead of waiting for the crowd to get quiet, they just start praying and inevitably, a shhh and side slap hitting fest goes across the audience that tells people to shut up, somebody up front is pretending to pray so you all will stop talking.

ok... I could go on... but it's getting depressing since I've been guilty of almost all of these a time or two.

I think I'm going to stop blogging and go pray. I surely need it.

Good Things Come in Small Groups:
25 Years of Discipling Men

by Steve Hixon

Hope for the deep-fried: an alternative to leadership burnout

I was only 24 years old. I had been a Christian for about 6 years and was close to burning out. I doubt I would've said so at the time, but during my summer pastoral internship at Peninsula Bible Church I desperately needed a reason to go on, ministry-wise. One day a staff member was innocently showing me a diagram depicting two different approaches to church work. "Wait a minute," I said. Before me was life and death, so to speak. In one picture the Christian "worker" (that would be me) ran around like a busy bee meeting every need, needing every meeting, being perfect, tirelessly teaching, planning, organizing, promoting - and then doing it all again the next week. The result? Some people were encouraged, helped, inspired - but mainly kept busy. The result for the "worker"? Exhaustion. I had assumed this was the only way to go; anything less was simply a lack of dedication.

As more than one person has pointed out, the church often looks like a football game: 50,000 people in the bleachers, desperately needing of exercise, watching 22 people on the field who are desperately in need of rest.

In the diagram, the alternate snapshot of ministry seemed too good to be true, probably illegal. It showed the "worker" doing relatively few things, but doing them well and enjoying them, and delegating the rest of the activities to the rest of the people, who were somehow supernaturally gifted to do and enjoy those things. The spectator-player dichotomy was gone; everyone was involved somehow. That was a defining moment for me. I can remember thinking, "If this is true, there's hope."

There's a famous scene in the movie *City Slickers* where Billy Crystal is speaking with the old, grizzled, wizened cowboy Curly (Jack Palance) and wondering aloud about what's most important in life. Curly sticks up one finger and says with a knowing grin, "One thing." It's a classic movie moment, because it speaks to a need we all have. Find that one thing you're called to do, and do it with all your heart.

But - what's the one thing? Somebody please tell me!

Equipping: What leaders are called to do

Fortunately, Ephesians chapter four shows spiritual leaders what the "one thing" is. In verses 11 through 13, Paul writes that the reason God "gave" leaders to the church was to "prepare God's people for works of ministry." The original word is "equip." That's the one true thing. Leaders (often called "ministers," which perpetuates the misconception) aren't supposed to do the whole ministry. Leaders are given and called by God to *equip the body of Christ* to do ministry.

"It was he who gave some to be apostles, some to be prophets, some to be evangelists, and some to be pastors and teachers, to prepare [equip] God's people for works of service, so that the body of Christ may be built up, until we all reach unity in the faith and in the knowledge of the Son of God and become mature, attaining to the whole measure of the fullness of Christ." (Ephesians 4:11-13, NIV)

Now, finding out what kind of equipment people need and how to give it to them, takes some thinking. After all, what does an "equipped" person look like?

For most of the 80's my wife and I ran a fairly large singles ministry. (Not a group for fairly large *people;* I mean a fairly large *group!*) It was one of the best and richest times in our lives. Constantly looking for the latest, greatest, cutting edge social event, we decided to take a bunch of people backpacking in Colorado. The sheepish volunteers met one evening and confessed that they had no more hiking equipment than their own youthful enthusiasm. We told them, fine - buy some boots and JSU – "just show up." We drove all day and night from Dallas, Texas to Wilderness Ranch in Creede, Colorado, where we were herded into a huge lodge, and told to sit down in a big circle. Expecting a lecture, we were surprised that the Ranch leaders didn't really talk all that much. Instead, they simply dumped a ton of stuff in the middle of the floor and began methodically distributing pieces to us novice campers - backpacks, stoves, tents, utensils, dried-food packets, parkas. An hour later we weren't any more experienced - but we sure were equipped. And the good news was, we weren't expected to go "out there" alone - the leaders were going with us, thank God. They were used to hiking nine miles with a full pack, finding the trail, navigating to the elusive "Window" and "Pyramid" rock formations, detecting hypothermia, and digging the BIFF (bathroom in forest floor). The leaders didn't do everything, and we didn't want them to. We would've been bored if they did. What we wanted, and desperately needed, was their encouragement, their expertise, and their training in how to use the equipment we'd been given.

What if spiritual leaders did the same?

One of the surprising things about ministry is how many leaders don't know about this life-saving principle. And what's even more surprising is that once they hear about it, once it's shown to them, their response is often, "That's nice, but I don't have time." Speaking before a group of dozens of pastors in Romania, I talked about this concept and watched them nod their heads. But in small groups, they confided, "I'm responsible for four churches in four different towns. I can barely keep going. My wife says she never sees me. How can I possibly find time to mentor, to disciple men? And if I did, what would I do?"

How could a leader be "too busy" to do their most important job? I guess the same way that I as a parent was often too busy to spend quality time with my kids. I wasn't doing bad things, I just let the loud cry of urgent things drown out the whisper of the more crucial things. Let's be honest; have you ever been to a pastor's conference? It's often one of the most competitive gatherings imaginable. What sounds cooler and more impressive: "Yeah, we doubled our budget last year, and now we're in the middle of a multi-million-dollar building campaign to accommodate all the people we're turning away," or "I meet with a bunch of messed-up guys every Thursday, and it's the most exciting thing I do." Don't get me wrong; the corporate side of church life is absolutely necessary. It's just that it's easy to be lured into a mindset where that's all there is.

Ron Ritchie & the Timothy Experience

During that same early internship, the summer of 1977, the first thing I was told was to go around and find out what all the staff people did. Just finding them was hard enough. That year PBC had 13 pastors, so the task pretty much filled up my day-timer. By far the most colorful and potentially deranged pastor was a guy named Ron, who ran the Careers ministry. He fit right into the 70's Bay Area ex-hippie culture: semi-long hair, beard, sunglasses, and jeans. To be honest, he was a little scary. Hardly your Dallas Seminary type, (actually he'd almost gotten thrown out of DTS for being a bit too authentic, but that's another story). But he wasn't quite as hang--loose as he appeared. He seemed unusually busy, but not the normal hectic-busy. More like purposeful--busy. I asked if he would show me what he did to train his leaders, and he led me into a room that revolved around a carefully-set table. But instead of plates, condiments and food it was full of notebooks, handouts and Bibles. "This is where my Timothys meet every Wednesday night," he said.

"What the heck is a "Timothy?" I silently wondered, but nodded knowingly.

Sensing my carefully covered-up confusion, he explained. "Jesus prayed all night asking the Father which guys, which disciples, to invest in. He poured his life into those men, and eventually he called them friends and brothers. Later, Paul trained a guy named Timothy. So every year I start praying and looking for men who are spiritually hungry. When I find a bunch of them, I send out a letter describing what I want to do with them, and asking them to consider it and respond by a certain date."

"We meet here every week for a year. I teach them how to understand the Bible, how to dig and discover truths for themselves, how to teach one another, how to find and develop their spiritual gifts, how to share their faith. They come prepared. We spend a couple hours in here studying, and then we all go out to dinner at a local restaurant."

"Out to dinner?" I asked.

"Yeah, because it's more than just knowledge; it's relationships. I want to see how they interact with each other, how they treat the waitress, if they actually care about people or just like to talk about it."

"Doesn't that get kind of expensive?" was my profound response.

Ron just stared at me.

That conversation pretty much stuck with me. Another defining moment, I guess you could say. So, when I had graduated from seminary and started into my first ministry, I thought, I think I'll do what Ron did.

The first few years and groups were pretty bumpy, full of gaffes and goofiness, a catalogue of dysfunction, and when they were over, I was usually thinking, "Duh! Why'd

I do it that way? Why didn't we try this?" And then the next group would get a little bit better; and the next one a little better yet. That was 25 years and almost as many groups ago.

I gradually came to the conclusion that they were worth it. They were messy, they were frustrating at times, the results were hard to quantify, but I felt a deepening conviction: this thing is worth it. I began to realize that when I didn't have a group, I really missed it. I also noticed that I was happiest getting in my car at 6 a.m. to drive to whatever restaurant my current group was meeting in. I loved watching the guys straggle in, sleepy but open to whatever God might do that morning, in that sacred time. And when I would drive away, I felt full of life. I couldn't imagine <u>not</u> doing this.

Befriend & impart: the essence of discipleship

So, what is the essence of discipleship? Paul talks about passing on what we've come to believe, and "passing it on" well enough that the learner can pass it on to someone else, and on and on through the succeeding generations.

You have heard me teach things that have been confirmed by many reliable witnesses. Now teach these truths to other trustworthy people who will be able to pass them on to others. (2 Timothy 2:2, NLT)

I've probably been on 50 weekend retreats, and the details tend to run together in my memory, but a few classic moments stand out. One autumn weekend we coerced most of the leaders in our church into getting away to the east Texas pine woods for a couple nights, and we asked Dave Roper, a seasoned pastor, to come and speak to us. Dave's pretty low-key, but he commands respect with his unique blend of scholarship and wisdom, and something he said almost off-the-cuff has stuck with me ever since I heard it that day. In his unassuming style, he told us that the essence of discipleship could be condensed into two words: "befriend and impart." Develop relationships, and then teach whatever you know that meets a spiritual need the other person has. I realized that often I did one or the other, but usually not both. I would try to teach someone spiritual truths without really earning the right to speak. As the old saying goes, people don't care how much you know until they know how much you care. And then other times I would make friends, but not really speak anything significant into their lives. Befriend and impart. Is there any

simpler or more accurate way to describe what Jesus did with people, especially the disciples?

Why small groups?

In the Great Commission, Jesus clearly told his followers that their main job was to make disciples (Matthew 29:28).

Then Jesus came to them and said, "All authority in heaven and on earth has been given to me. Therefore go and make disciples of all nations, baptizing them in the name of the Father and of the Son and of the Holy Spirit, and teaching them to obey everything I have commanded you. And surely I am with you always, to the very end of the age. (Matthew 28:18-20)

However, like many New Testament commands, this one was left purposely vague in terms of exactly how it was to be applied. I think this is God's wisdom, allowing for different personalities in different times and places to be creative under the leadership of the Holy Spirit. Should we make disciples simply by writing things down in documents and telling people to read them? I once had a seminary professor who, being critical of the "one-on-one" style of ministry that was popular at the time, said, "Yeah, I believe in one-on-one. One book, on one man!" Needless to say, he wasn't the most relational teacher on campus.

Is one-on-one really best? Should an older, more mature believer meet individually with a novice Christian for spiritual guidance? This has been effective in many situations. Or should you add one more body, like the "triad" approach that some people prefer? In that case, an older leader doubles his or her impact by teaching two at a time.

You can probably guess that I will say that any of these systems are valid as long as they actually work. Personally, I prefer small groups. Perhaps it's because of my own personal wiring, maybe it has to do with some very positive early experiences I had with groups. I think groups have more potential for disaster and dysfunction, but like I said before, I'm convinced that they also have tremendous possibilities for growth, based on the sheer multi-faceted dynamics of interaction and activity. Learning is multiplied when I listen to six men voice their observations on a passage of the Bible. I can ask a man to teach a verse of Scripture to the group, and he's not just talking back to me. We experience a microcosm of the Body of Christ in a small group, with a wide variety of personality types and a range of spiritual gifts. Plus, as a pastor I couldn't always carve out 2 hours a week for six different guys, but I could easily arrange to meet with a group of six guys for 2 hours.

Another reason I like groups is because new believers are impressionable. How often, in a one-one-one context, does the novice Christian assume, even subconsciously, that he should become exactly like the teacher, especially if the teacher has an A-type personality? What if the "learner" is a B-type? They can spend years trying to measure up to the stature of their omni-gifted "discipler." But in a healthy group, strong personalities lose some of their unhealthy tendencies, as they are forced to serve and submit to others.

How big should a group get; what's the perfect size? What a silly question. Of course it's 13, because Jesus had 12 disciples. OK, just kidding. Again, it's up to you. For a while I didn't want anything larger than 6 or 7, but then one year we ended up with ten guys, and I loved it. Of course there are trade-offs, since time is limited, and the larger the group, the less time each person can speak, and shy people can have a tendency to hide. In a larger group, the leader needs to be more proactive about guiding the discussion, making sure no one dominates and no one gets lost in the shuffle.

One way to help this is by having a co-leader. Recently I started a group with another man for whom I have tremendous respect. We see eye-to-eye on our goals and values, but we have different gifts and approaches, making a good leadership team combination. But we need to stay in touch to stay on track, so we talk weekly about how we felt the last meeting went, what we want to do next time, how the time will be divided, etc. If we don't communicate, we'll frustrate ourselves or cancel each other out. But the camaraderie of it feels good to me. Like the Lewis & Clark expedition (a great study in leaders, by the way), I think everyone benefits from multiple leadership.

Covenant - negotiating for success at the start

Small groups tend to follow some very predictable patterns, most of which have been carefully studied and documented (see *Growth Groups*, by Michael Dibbert for example). They have foreseeable life cycle stages and relational dynamics. For instance, most of the groups I have been in have exhibited some or all of the following characteristics:

- Initial excitement in the first few meetings, creating an unrealistic and transient euphoria
- Several months into the group, unmet expectations surface, stemming from misunderstandings or never-expressed desires
- Waning energy starting in the middle stages of the group, people backing off their involvement or commitment
- In the end, the group simply fades away as members eventually have to leave. Dominant personalities hog the time with long-winded off-subject diatribes
- Shy personalities only speak when they're sure of what to say, or who are afraid of being wrong
- People start not showing up, or showing up unprepared, leading more conscientious members to wonder if it's really worth it to spend time studying in advance
- Someone dares to share something really risky and vulnerable, and their "offering" is shut down, preached at, trivialized, spiritualized or worse, ignored - creating a glass ceiling which severely limits authenticity

How to solve these problems? Here's what I've found (everyone lean in to listen to the magic formula) - you can't! At least not completely, especially in a fallen world where people abound with idiosyncrasies, personality defects, defense mechanisms. As John Ortberg states in the title of his book, *Everybody's Normal Until You Get to Know Them!* And as pastors love to quip, "Ministry is great; it's just the people I can't stand." Ministry will always be messy; however (and here's the hope), apart from leadership skills, one helpful tool is the group covenant. It's not so much the document itself that solves problems, but the disciplined process of discussing group dysfunction before it even starts. Why is it that most engaged couples don't get pre-marital counseling? Because they don't feel like they need it. After all, they're happy! Every time a young couple asks to me to perform their wedding ceremony, I inquire how they're handling conflict in their relationship. Sheepishly, but proudly, they often announce, "You know, we've never even had a fight!" My instinct is to say, "Run for the hills; you're clueless." It's the couples who can name their areas of potential disagreement that I feel good about.

Likewise, the initial energy and euphoria of a new small group gives the false impression that there will be no problems. Look how much we like each other! No one will ever be late, rude, unprepared, uncaring, loud, manipulative, insecure, or (you fill in the blank.)

Therefore, what I've done is a kind of reverse-engineering for group life. I try to think through all the things that have damaged, derailed or destroyed groups in the past. Then I create a group covenant document that I hand out at or before the first meeting, and we spend a significant amount of time going over it in every detail. A covenant is a description of how we want to conduct ourselves as a group, a picture of how we want to treat one another. I try to explain why each point is important, and give examples of past mistakes (especially ones I've made). I ask the guys to respond, so I know whether they "get it" or not. A sample of the issues:

- Showing up: What it does to the group if somebody is 15 minutes late every time
- What happens here, stays here: Why confidentiality is critical to people feeling safe telling their stories
- Why we try to balance knowledge and practical life-application, personal sharing and serious study
- Doing our homework: What happens if people don't prepare but just "wing-it," spouting popular conventional wisdom rather than truth they've discovered on their own
- Caring by paying attention: The importance and skill of listening to others in the group

A group covenant is like marriage vows. Do I perfectly love my wife? No, but that's the direction I want to move in. The covenant is something I can come back to and review time and again (which is actually a pretty good thing to do, maybe every couple months), to reaffirm what I initially agreed to pursue. And there's got to be an atmosphere of grace; we'll all screw up from time to time. A covenant is not a license to be a group Nazi, but it's a chance, like good pre-marital counseling, to talk about problems before they surface in real life. That way emotions, frustration and anger don't rule. How many times have you been in a group and, after several mediocre meetings, someone finally says, "Susy, you're kinda bugging me. By the time you're finished talking, there's no room left for anyone else." "Hmmm - so, how long has this been bothering you?"

"For two years."

(Steve Hixon's version of a Group Covenant is on page 82.)

Closure - ending well is important

Relationships don't have to end, but groups usually do. And just as it's important to start well, it's equally important to end well. Surprisingly, most groups just fade away with little or no fanfare. But with just a little foresight and planning, a group can send itself off into the proverbial sunset with a great celebration. After all, you've invested a lot of time and effort in this, so why not take a moment to remember the best? Closure is a way to say thanks to God and to each other for the gift of friendship and brotherhood.

Think about what Jesus did. He alone knew that the end was near. Most of the disciples probably didn't even realize that the Last Supper was the *last* supper, but he did, and he made sure it was a special evening. I'm sure the men reminisced about the three years they had spent together. Perhaps there was laughter. And Jesus seized the moment to give his great command - that they prove their commitment to him by choosing to love each other. He gave them an object lesson illustrating his own love for them, a parting gift that they would never forget. He washed their feet.

Be as creative as you want. What's most important is that, if possible, 100% of the group is present. Ask them to show up having thought through the time you had together. Last summer our group celebrated our study of the Psalms by each person bringing an expression of what they'd learned. People wrote psalms, poems, drew pictures, created collages, made slideshows. Some were hilariously funny, others were achingly poignant. It was a great evening and it honored and elevated the weeks we had spent together, acknowledged that it had been worth it, that it meant something to us, that it was another strong brick in the building of our faith. Take a picture of the group, and give each person a copy. Who knows if or when, in this hectic world, that same set of people will ever be together again this side of heaven.

On a larger scale, at one church we took the small group discipleship concept and created a program out of it. We spent months training leaders, then unleashed them upon men and women who had signed up for groups. We shepherded the leaders by meeting with them regularly, and at the end of the year we had a big banquet at a local hotel for the hundreds who had participated, and spent the evening sharing our experiences with laughter and tears. I recall that perhaps the greatest impact was felt by the spouses who attended but hadn't been in groups yet. Listening to the authentic stories that night, many of them sensed a spiritual awakening in their own hearts.

Core curriculum: what to study?

Good question! While there are no perfect answers, there are some bad or at least mediocre ones. The curriculum for the group is the diet. Will it be nutritional or junk food?

My bias is that the Bible is critical to discipleship. Many groups will decide to read the latest popular Christian bestseller, but my experience is that groups based on these books usually last a few meetings, and then quickly start to lose steam. Christian books aren't inspired, the Bible is. The Holy Spirit only promises to inhabit one book; there's only one written Word. Someone once told me that the Bible is the track that the Spirit runs on. So if your goal is to produce disciples who own, understand, and can teach what they believe, what better curriculum than the Scriptures themselves?

Having said that, what do you do, read and explain the whole Bible? No group has time for that, and besides, that's the lifetime pursuit of every believer. In the mid-1980's, some friends and I sat down to try to answer this question. What do believers need to know? If we only have 6 months or a year with a person, how do we equip them? What do they need? We concluded that they didn't just need data; they needed essential concepts, or principles. They could spend the rest of their lives gathering Biblical facts. We realized that while there is an enormous amount off actual information in the Bible, there are relatively few, or at least a manageable number of principles. What principles do I really need to grasp to live the Christian life?

We forced ourselves to make a huge list, and then whittle it down to fifteen. Why fifteen, is that a magic number? Absolutely not. We just picked it out of thin air. But we realized that often groups may only meet for six months to a year, and it seemed to fit. Also, we decided to use John 15 as a template. In that passage, Jesus is speaking to his men on their last night together. He mentions three vital relationships that they needed to understand: their relationship with God, with each other, and with the world. And so we chose to organize our principles around those three relationships. We limited ourselves to five principles for each relationship, making fifteen in all. There could just as easily be 12, or 18. But if I spend a year with young

believers, at the end of that experience I want them to have a grasp on who God is, and who they are in relationship to Him. I want them to understand the importance of the body of Christ, since Christians are not designed to be lone rangers, but living out their faith in the midst of a believing community. And finally, I want them to know that there is a world system, and there is spiritual warfare, and that God wants us to operate in the world as His ambassadors, reaching out to those who are dying spiritually, offering the true bread of life to hungry people; and not arrogantly, but graciously, as beggars helping other beggars.

That's the core curriculum. There are plenty on the market, and you may have found or created something that really works for you. That's great. Revolving around that core, I want to also "impart" skills to the men in my group. Those skills are: how to study the Bible, how to teach a passage from the Bible, how to answer tough questions about their faith (apologetics), how to discover and develop your spiritual gifts, how to share your faith with other people. (As one friend of mine likes to say, when someone asks him what he does for a living, "I talk to people about Jesus when they're interested. Are you interested?")

If time permits, I also like to introduce guys to some great, short books on critical topics. I emphasize "short" because there's no quicker way to quench someone's interest in a topic than by giving them a 900 page tome that will serve as a great doorstop. (In seminary I was told to buy *The Attributes of God* by Stephen Charnock, a 17th -century Puritan who evidently had some time on his hands. It's enormous, almost 1200 pages. I never got past page 6, but I felt all holy while I was buying it!) Some of my favorites include:

- *More Than a Carpenter* by Josh McDowell (apologetics)
- *The Master Plan of Evangelism* by Robert Coleman (how Jesus trained his men)
- *Too Busy Not to Pray* by Bill Hybels (prayer, duh)
- *Messy Spirituality* by Mike Yaconelli (grace)
- *The Jesus I Never Knew* by Philip Yancey (the life of Christ)

I'm also constantly on the lookout for great short articles on essential topics. Some of the best brief treatments of

[handwritten note: LIFE STORY TURN THEM INTO A FAMILY. DON'T BE IN A HURRY.]

difficult subjects come from C.S. Lewis, John Stott, J.I. Packer, Francis Schaeffer, Ray Stedman, Philip Yancey, Dietrich Bonhoeffer, Henri Nouwen. I love to introduce men to great authors, who will become trustworthy wells of wisdom from which to draw for the rest of their lives.

Discipleship in Action: Real-Life Stories

Well, I've described all this in theory. But what does it look like in real life?

Can I share some snapshots with you? If I had a picture album from all my discipleship groups, the following moments would definitely be keepers.

Frank's story

Frank was rocking like a maniac, and it looked like he was starting to sweat. Glancing around, I locked eyes with Ken, and we both thought, "What the heck?" Everyone had put together a "life map," a graphic representation of the significant people and defining moments in their lives. It was Frank's turn to tell his story, to share with us whatever he wanted to from his whole life. It didn't seem like it ought to be this hard, and it wasn't like he was the first in our group to do it. The rocking chair he was in actually began to skip across the hardwood floor as he recounted his early years growing up in Florida. Finally I couldn't take it any more, I had to ask, "Frank, do you realize that you and that chair are about to take off? Are you nervous, or what?" I'll never forget what he said next.

"No one's ever heard this before."

"What do you mean, this part of your story?"

"No - any part. I've never told my life story to anyone."

"But…weren't you married for a several years?"

"Like I said, I've never told anyone."

In the book, *The Friendless American Male*, David Smith says, "Women seem to have a monopoly on meaningful, intimate relationships…Men have friendships which relate to work or play, but seldom go beyond the surface…"

Ben's serious challenge

Before, and after Ben became a follower of Christ, he spent hours and hours each week in smoke-filled rooms, playing guitar and mandolin for one of the best Irish bands in Texas. Somehow he came into a relationship with God and appeared on the horizon of our little church, and then made his way into my guys' group. Ben's major contribution was that he taught us to take each other seriously. From the very first meeting, he let us know. "Look, if I'm going to show up, I want you to show up too, and I want you to be on time. Don't make me sit around waiting for you! And if I study and prepare the lesson, I don't want you to show up with a blank piece of paper." Well, that woke everyone up! I smiled to myself, thinking he'd said it better than I could have, and coming from a group member, it carried a lot of weight. After all, he was just a volunteer. He wasn't paid to be good, like me. He was just good for nothing. (OK, I couldn't resist.)

Ben let us know that this was a critical, unique time in his life, and our lives, and he didn't want to mess around. He really wanted to grow. He had only recently come to accept Jesus Christ, and he was eager to see real life change. Thankfully he hadn't lapsed into the kind of go-to-Bible-study mentality that was more an inoculation against change than an authentic adventure.

The opportunity came a few weeks into the group. "I want to quit smoking and I need your help," he announced. "I've tried five times before and it never works. We just found out that Susan is pregnant, and I always said I wanted to quit before we had our first child."

We nodded in agreement, but nobody really knew what to say next. There's no magic formula for things like this. But out of the blue Sam had an idea, "Look," he said, "there are eight of us. Why don't we each pick a day this coming week and fast and pray for Ben?"

"Fast - like, don't eat for a whole day?" someone verbalized what we were all thinking. "A whole day just for Ben? I mean, maybe he's worth skipping lunch for, but…!"

But we all did it, and when the next meeting rolled around, we desperately wanted to know what had happened. After all, we'd made pretty major investments, especially for guys! All eyes were on Ben. "Well…?"

"You're not gonna believe this. I quit! I just stopped and never turned back. It's the only time it's ever worked."

And it's still working for Ben. The point is not that smoking is the unforgivable sin, but that we did something together, and saw God work, saw an answer to prayer. It made us all want to pray more, and it bound us together as brothers.

The value of time spent together

Our kids spent 18 years each living in our home, but I

can't remember many individual days or nights. The mundane blends together. The ones that stand out are the ones that were different somehow. The time my son and I spent the night in a friend's cabin, eating pizza and playing games, just the two of us; the Mondays when my second-grade daughter and I had breakfast together because a special program allowed her to go to school an hour late; the afternoon my younger daughter and I drove our ailing golden retriever to the vet, and came back alone, never to see him again.

Likewise, I don't recall the normal meetings with the guys, but the unusual times. Like the time we packed up the cars and drove to a cabin in the mountains for a night, fishing in the nearby stream, riding bikes down a trail at breakneck speed, whitewater rafting and grinning like idiots as we careened through the class-4 rapids. It was over too quickly, but I still have that photograph.

Or the time we all pitched in to put a new roof on a church member's house; she had the materials, but no husband, and no money, and no friends to do it. So we found out and volunteered. I'd never nailed a single shingle before, and I prayed to God that the roof would last despite my incompetence. I can still see us, scattered across the top of that little house, like rats on a sinking ship. But somehow it worked, and again, we did it together. It was something tangible, a real person's real need met.

John's defining moment

John would always say what was on his mind, which was one of the reasons I liked him. "I swear, sometimes I don't even know if I'm a Christian or not," he blurted one morning. "I mean, I've been in this church forever, but some days I just wonder."

Hmm. How to respond to this honesty? "Well," I said, "do you feel like you believe these things we're studying?"

"Yeah, but then I screw up and doubt that I've ever really changed. It's like I'm in a spiritual revolving door."

I secretly wondered how many men and women feel the same way, not knowing that most basic truth - am I, or am I not? Am I forgiven, or do I need to do something else?

John went on, "Would you guys do something?"

"Sure. What?"

"Would you sign a piece of paper saying you witnessed my confession?"

In all the years of meeting with guys, I'd never even thought of such a thing. According to his wish, I asked John, "Do you believe that you need a savior, and that Jesus offered himself for you and paid for your sin? Do you accept his free gift? Is that where your heart is?"

"Yes, absolutely," John replied, wholeheartedly.

So we passed around a piece of paper and signed it, saying we'd witnessed the declaration of John's heart, and that we stood together with him as brothers in Christ. I think he took it to Kinko's the next day and had it laminated, and now he keeps it in his wallet. "Whenever I have doubts, I pull out that card," he said a few weeks later, with a twinkle in his eye. "It's like a confirmation."

Bob's stunning revelation

I glanced at the clock. Dang, not much time left. Our practice was to study for an hour and leave the last 30 minutes for one guy to share whatever he wanted from his life map. He could share deep or shallow, where he was born or went to grade school, or the most painful trauma of his life. Certainly today, I thought, with ten minutes left, Bob won't want to open up. I wouldn't. I wouldn't risk baring my soul, only to have guys look at their watches and say, sorry, I'm late for work. It was the perfect excuse to be superficial.

Bob hesitated, and his lip began to quiver. What's going on inside him? I wondered.

He began slowly, but soon it became apparent that this was not going to be anything superficial. We were glued to his words, not really wanting to hear them, but unable to turn away as he recounted the horror of an escalating and destructive pattern of sin in his not-so-long-ago past. Tears began to flow, and not just from Bob. Inside, each of us thought, "That could so easily be me. God don't let me do that. Please don't let that happen." Thankfully, Bob's story took a hopeful, positive turn, but it wasn't completely over with yet, and there were no easy answers. Yet there was God's grace, and there was significant healing. He paused. In the wake of his story we all sat stunned. What do you do next? Just disband for the morning and say, "Well, have a nice day?"

I wasn't sure what to say, but I thanked Bob for trusting us with this bombshell, and then I looked around at the group and quietly asked, "What did you hear from Bob? What does it mean to you?" There was silence for a few seconds, no one sure what was appropriate; like funeral mourners, not wanting to say something amazingly stupid. Finally Jerry summed it up so well. He smiled and said,

"Transformation is a beautiful thing." We all silently agreed; it was the perfect thing to say. Bob was being transformed. God was taking ugliness and creating beauty, an ugliness we all knew we had inside, and a beauty we all desperately wanted. Bob was being transformed, and we got to watch. It reminded me of what I think might be Jesus' favorite Old Testament passage, because he quoted it when he was asked to speak in his hometown. Isaiah 61:1-3 describes the kind of transformation God loves to create:

> **The Lord has sent me to bind up the brokenhearted,**
> **to proclaim freedom for the captives**
> **and release from darkness for the prisoners,**
> **...to comfort all who mourn,**
> **to bestow on them**
> **a crown of beauty instead of ashes, the oil of gladness instead of mourning,**
> **and a garment of praise instead of a spirit of despair.**
> **They will be called oaks of righteousness, a planting of the LORD**
> **for the display of his splendor.**

And once again, this time in the New Testament:

> **And so we are transfigured much like the Messiah, our lives gradually becoming brighter and more beautiful as God enters our lives and we become like him.** (2 Cor. 3:18, The Message)

Summing it all up

Well, I could go on and on, mainly because the Spirit of God is going on and on, as one church puts it, "transforming irreligious people into fully-devoted followers of Christ." Thank God He does. And the weird thing is - He wants you and me to be involved. He wants your hands, your feet, your eyes, your words; your unique, unusual, special wiring. And the amazing thing, the glory of the ministry, as D. Martyn Lloyd-Jones used to say, is that *"you never know what's going to happen."*

℘ ℭ

Steve Hixon and I co-pastored at Fellowship Bible Church in Colorado Springs (1997-2000). We are both graduates of Dallas Theological Seminary and are committed to our Lord Jesus' command, "In your going make disciples..." When we first teamed up at FBC we began discipling the elders (and potential elders) who were the spiritual leaders of the church, but who had never been discipled.

I wanted to include Steve's discipleship material to show you how we both use many of the same principles and materials, and yet incorporate our different personalities and spiritual gifts.

Our heart's desire is that you will seriously consider discipling other believers by beginning where you are in your life right now with Jesus, and then growing in your understanding of our Lord's command.

Ron R. Ritchie

Used with permission.

DISCIPLESHIP GROUP COVENANT

Signed: _____

This covenant is an agreement among brothers in Christ as to how we want to treat one another and how we desire to function as a group. It is a commitment we make as to our intentions, and like all commitments in Christ, we fully realize that we must rely upon the Holy Spirit for any of this to happen!

For as long as I am in this group, I will make every attempt to...

- **Show up** on time unless I absolutely can't make it, in which case I'll call one of the guys in the group to let them know ahead of time.

  "Simply let your 'Yes' be 'Yes,' and your 'No,' 'No'... (Matt. 5:37)

- **Be prepared** by studying the material for the week to the best of my ability and time my schedule and other commitments allow.

  "Do your best to present yourself to God as one approved, a workman who does not need to be ashamed and who correctly handles the word of truth." (2 Tim. 2:15)

- **Contribute** to the group discussion, believing that healthy interaction requires everyone's input and that each member has something special to offer.

  "Now you are the body of Christ, and each one of you is a part of it." (1 Cor. 12:27)

- **Be honest** about how I am doing in my life and in my walk with God. Complete vulnerability cannot be forced and is not always wise, but I desire to honor these brothers by letting them know what's going on in my life.

  "Kings take pleasure in honest lips; they value a man who speaks the truth." (Prov. 16: 13)

- **Keep my relationships** with others in the group in good repair. If I have a problem with someone, I will *try* to work it out with them rather than gossiping, putting them down or ignoring the issue.

  "If your brother sins against you, go and show him his fault, just between the two of you. If he listens to you, you have won your brother over." (Matt. 18:15)

- **Be emotionally available** to the guys in the group - that is, care about them as brothers, rejoicing when good things come into their lives and showing appropriate concern when times are tough.

  "Rejoice with those who rejoice; mourn with those who mourn." (Rom. 12:15)

  "If one part suffers, every part suffers with it; if one part is honored, every part rejoices with it." (1 Cor. 12:26)

  "Therefore confess your sins to each other and pray for each other so that you may be healed." (James 5:16)

- **Be confidential** about things that others share within the group.

  "With the tongue we praise our Lord and Father, and with it we curse men, who have been made in God's likeness. Out of the same mouth come praise and cursing. My brothers, this should not be." (James 3:9, 10)

- **Discover and use my spiritual gifts** in whatever setting God has planned for me.

  "For we are God's workmanship, created in Christ Jesus to do good works, which God prepared in advance for us to do." (Eph. 2: 10)

  "Each one should use whatever gift he has received to serve others..." (1 Peter 4:10)

The Inductive Study Guide

The study material on the following pages was taken from my inductive study guide entitled:

Free At Last! - The New Covenant

We've chosen two chapters to give you some practical experience in using the *inductive study method* so you help disciple others on how to study the Word of God. Our desire is to provide each Timothy with both the *fishing equipment* and lessons on *how to fish* through the scriptures, and to use that knowledge for the rest of their lives as they fish for men and women and lead them into the Kingdom of God.

Jesus said to his disciples who he found casting a net in the Sea of Galilee, "Come after Me and I will make you to become fishers of men." - Mark 1:17

"...make disciples of all the nations, baptizing them in the name of the Father and the Son and the Holy Spirit, teaching them to observe all that I commanded you; and lo, I am with you always, even to the end of the age..." - Matthew 28:19-20

"Be diligent to present yourself approved to God as a workman who does not need to be ashamed, accurately handling the word of truth." - 2 Timothy 2:15

"All Scripture is inspired by God and profitable for teaching, for reproof, for correction, for training in righteousness; so that the man of God may be adequate, equipped for every good work." - 2 Timothy 3:16-17

Free at Last!

"So if the Son makes you free,
you will be free indeed"
Jesus

Ron R. Ritchie

THE NEW COVENANT, A LIFE STYLE
Inductive Study Guide
© 1976 Ron R. Ritchie
© 2003 Peninsula Bible Church
Published by Discovery Publishing, the publications ministry of Peninsula Bible
Church, 3505 Middlefield Road, Palo Alto, CA 94306

THE
NEW COVENANT

LESSON PLAN

THE
NEW COVENANT

COMFORT IN SUFFERING
2 CORINTHIANS 1:1 – 2:12

THE CITY   CORINTH: A seaport city (think of San Francisco) on the southern tip of Greece. It had a thriving population of 500,000 in 54 AD. The city was known as a cradle of pleasure and a showplace of architectural beauty. It was also the hub of the civilized world, both socially as well as economically. Its people were characterized by a lack of aristocracy, tradition and loyalty to the city fathers. In fact, because of the cosmopolitan and corrupt makeup of the city, the people were filled with a competitive spirit and loose morals.

THE PEOPLE   Through her gates passed every race, color and tribe; the great and the small, rich and poor, as well as the strong and weak. It was a city filled with philosophers, artists, merchants, politicians, and priests, as well as its share of fornicators, idolaters, adulterers, male and female prostitutes, homosexuals, thieves, drunkards, slanderers and swindlers, who thrived on the tourist trade. The very word "Corinthian" was synonymous with drunkenness and immorality. During Paul's time (50's AD) there was one source of evil in Corinth of which the whole western world took note: above the city there towered the hill of the Acropolis. (It can still be seen today as Corinth lays in ruins at its feet). On the top of this hill stood the great temple of Aphrodite, the goddess of Love. To that temple were attached one thousand priestesses who were religious prostitutes. At night, they would descend from their nest and come into the city. As they walked, the hobnails in the soles of their sandals spelled out "follow me" in the dust. It was here that they offered their favors to the tourists. It eventually became a Greek proverb that "it is not every man who can afford to journey to Corinth."

THE TENTMAKER	Around 50 – 51 AD a small Jewish man with a Roman passport came to town and walked through this marvelous city. He was a tentmaker by trade. In order to maintain his livelihood, he went down to the marketplace and inquired about some possibilities of work. It was during this time he met a Jewish couple name Aquila and Priscilla who were involved in the same trade and loved the Lord Jesus Christ. Together these three worked and preached the gospel for some two years and were able to lay the foundation for a Christian church in the midst of "Vanity Fair." This tentmaker was Paul of Tarsus.
THE BELIEVERS	Keep in mind that these believers were from different Gentile and Pagan backgrounds. Remember also that there existed a marked social and economic difference as well as a value system that encouraged "love of pleasure" and a "party spirit."Two pressure points seemed to underline all the problems the Corinthian Christians were having (as recorded in 1 and 2 Corinthians): the CULTURE and their GREEK CHARACTER.

CULTURE		CHARACTER		RESULT
1. Commercial Cosmopolitan	+	Party Spirit	=	Rivalry
2. Corruption	+	Love of Pleasure	=	Immorality

THE CHURCH	After some two years of teaching, Paul went east across the Aegean Sea to Ephesus in Asia. While he was there, he heard that several problems had arisen in the Corinthian church. He wrote 1 Corinthians to correct some of the divisiveness and immorality that was slowly creeping into the believers' lives. After writing this letter, he discovered a group of Jews opposing his authority as an apostle known as Judaizers. They hounded Paul's ministry constantly, insisting that "unless you are circumcised according to the custom of Moses, you cannot be saved" (Acts 15:1). Paul returned to Corinth, but found the Judaizers so well entrenched that he wasn't allowed to even teach in his own church.
	Paul then returned to Ephesus, wrote a new letter (now lost) and asked Titus to deliver it, and waited in Ephesus for an answer. While he waited, he continued to teach the gospel which was so successful that scores of men and women were coming to accept Jesus as Lord and Savior, and thus cutting into the idol-making trade within that city. The silversmiths started a riot and Paul was forced to leave town (Acts 19).
	He went north to the seaport of Troas, hoping he would meet Titus returning from Corinth with some news of their reaction to his letter but he didn't find Titus, so he went westward across the sea into Philippi, Greece and wrote 2 Corinthians.
DATE	Written by Paul from Philippi during 54 to 56 AD.

Inductive Bible Study

BE DILIGENT [an ever present command] TO PRESENT YOURSELF APPROVED TO GOD [not man] AS A WORKMAN [not a lazy man] WHO DOES NOT NEED TO BE ASHAMED, ACCURATELY HANDLING [a present lifestyle] THE WORD OF TRUTH. (2 Timothy 2:15 - NASB)

PURPOSE

FOR EVERYONE WHO PARTAKES ONLY OF MILK IS NOT ACCUSTOMED TO THE WORD OF RIGHTEOUSNESS, FOR HE IS AN INFANT. BUT SOLID FOOD IS [present lifestyle] FOR THE MATURE, WHO BECAUSE OF PRACTICE HAVE THEIR SENSES TRAINED TO DISCERN GOOD AND EVIL. (Heb. 5:13, 14 – NASB)

METHOD

INDUCTIVE BIBLE STUDY, a method that is basically an objective and impartable approach to Scripture, demands that the student put any section of the Word under the discipline of three basic steps that move from a general overview to particulars. Then and only then can you (the student) draw conclusions from those particulars.

INDUCTIVE BIBLE STUDY is designed to bring joy to the "digger." It is one thing to hear about a friend who found gold, it's quite another to discover the gold for yourself. The general subject is gold, and the particulars come as you ask certain questions— where, when, how, who, what, and why? After this process you can intelligently, objectively, and confidently discern the correct direction to take under the guidance of the Holy Spirit.

By the principles of OBSERVATION (What do I see?), INTERPRETATION (What does it mean in its immediate context?), and APPLICATION (What does it mean to me today?), a student, who is dependent on the Lord, through practice can soon become an independent "miner" of Biblical truth.

However, it is important to be aware of two errors that beset a student of the Word. First, taking everything secondhand from others; or secondly, refusing to take anything from others. We are a body, tied together under the leadership of Jesus Christ so Christ has given us a system of checks and balances that enable you (the student) to check your findings against other brothers and sisters' findings. You learn the differences between "fools gold" and the real thing by sharing your findings and allowing them to be evaluated by the Word, the Spirit, and the family of God.

TOOL BOOKS

The following are some basic tools necessary to have on hand for an enjoyable "dig."
- *A Bible*. Any version that is based on the original language. Avoid any paraphrase or loose translation as a basic tool.
- *A Bible Dictionary* offers lasting value because it handles every word mentioned in the Bible. ·
- *A Bible Concordance* enables you to find any verse in the Bible, so long as you can remember at least one word. It also lists every verse in the Bible for any given word.
- *A Bible Atlas*. Many Bible dictionaries have maps in the back, but it is also valuable to get a separate set of maps to keep nearby.

KEY

There are many ways to do <u>Inductive Bible Study,</u> but for the purpose of this study, we want to get you started in basic principles and hope that you will branch out on your own creative adventure. Complete one lesson per week. Add questions, take out ideas you don't agree with, and in time you will develop a lifestyle that will make Bible study a delight, and there will be no portion of scripture you will avoid. Now, read the entire book and do an overview chart (see below).

OVERVIEW CHART

Chapter	1-5	6-7	8-10	11-13
Subject	The ministry within the Church	Personal responsibility	Responsibilities toward others	Warning against false teachers

We will be studying 2 Corinthians 2:14-6:13 only, but see if you can give a title to the above chart that would summarize the whole book:

_____

TITLE

Go into the text now, line upon line, precept upon precept.

¹ CONTEXT?

- Date written
- Author
- Purpose
- Type of literature—
  prose, poetry, discourse, apocalyptic

- Culture
- Political events
- Contemporaries from
  secular history

- Main Purpose
- Cycle of events
- Major divisions
- Pressure points

² WHAT DOES IT SAY?	³ WHAT DOES IT MEAN?
Write out the verses you want to study so that you don't miss words or verb tenses, etc. Learn to really see words; be honest when you don't understand a word or phrase. Look for repetition of words, phrases; look for key words.	Here is where you learn to ask questions. Who, what, where, how, when, why? Who is speaking? Where is he going? What does he mean? How is he going? When is he going? Why is he going? What does this word mean? Use your Bible Atlas, Dictionaries, and Word Studies. Leave no stone unturned.

⁴ SUMMARIZE!

Put the parts all back together and see if you can come up with a statement that will summarize all that has been studied.

⁵ SPIRITUAL PRINCIPLES!

Since all Scripture (Old Testament and New Testament) is given to us for our instruction, in our process of maturity we should never read Scripture as history or literature, but, as in Ephesians, we should see and understand the historical context and then draw out the spiritual principles. (2 Timothy 3:16, 17)

Example: "But thanks be to God who always leads us in His triumph in Christ..."

I should always have a thankful heart because God will bring triumph out of an apparent failure. There is nothing that happens to me that is an accident, but God's hand is on everything.

⁶ SO WHAT?

- ❖ Whether you are studying the Old or New Testaments, you will discover that spiritual truths are never confined to any one time or culture, for man's nature is consistent.
- ❖ Ask yourself if the spiritual principles can be applied universally, nationally, locally, personally, or all of the above.
- ❖ Ask the Lord to give you the ability to incorporate these truths into your lifestyle.

NOTES

READ

The main thrust of our study will be found in 2 Corinthians 2:14 – 6:13. However, read 2 Corinthians 1:1–2:12 for an overview. Our first inductive Bible study will begin with 2 Corinthians 1:3-11.

GOD COMFORTS US IN OUR SUFFERING

Blessed be the God and Father of our Lord Jesus Christ, the Father of mercies and God of all comfort, who comforts us in all our affliction so that we will be able to comfort those who are in any affliction with the comfort with which we ourselves are comforted by God. For just as the sufferings of Christ are ours in abundance, so also our comfort is abundant through Christ. But if we are afflicted, it is for your comfort and salvation; or if we are comforted, it is for your comfort, which is effective in the patient enduring of the same sufferings which we also suffer; and our hope for you is firmly grounded, knowing that as you are sharers of our sufferings, so also you are sharers of our comfort. For we do not want you to be unaware, brethren, of our affliction which came to us in Asia, that we were burdened excessively, beyond our strength, so that we despaired even of life; indeed, we had the sentence of death within ourselves so that we would not trust in ourselves, but in God who raises the dead; who delivered us from so great a peril of death, and will deliver us, He on whom we have set our hope. And He will yet deliver us, you also joining in helping us through your prayers, so that thanks may be given by many persons on our behalf for the favor bestowed on us through the prayers of many. (2 Corinthians 1:3-11, NASB)

WHAT DOES IT SAY?	WHAT DID IT MEAN IN THE CORINTHIAN CONTEXT?
1:3 Blessed be the God and Father of our Lord Jesus Christ, the Father of mercies and God of all comfort….	Define the word "bless" (use a Bible dictionary): _____ _____ Who is to be blessed? _____ Why is He to be blessed (praised)? _____ _____ 1. _____ 2. _____ 3. _____ What does "Jesus" mean? _____ What does "Christ" mean? _____ Why is Jesus called *Lord*? _____ In view of the duty of the Son, how is it possible to speak of the God of our Lord Jesus Christ? The answer to this problem is to be found in the mediatorial office of Christ. God is not God of the Son as God, but His father. As a Mediator, however, the Son humbled Himself and in the incarnation assumed our human nature. As Mediator, He is our Lord Jesus Christ. God's anointed servant, the divine Son suffering as man for man and thereby bridging the gulf between man and God. In partaking of our nature the Mediator placed Himself in a position of dependence on God…." Philip E. Hughes, 2 Corinthians, p. 10 Read Philippians 2:5-11.

1:4

who comforts us

in all our affliction so

that we will be able to comfort those who are in any affliction...

1:5

For just as the sufferings of Christ are ours in abundance so also our comfort is abundant through Christ.

1:6

But if we are afflicted it is for your comfort and salvation;

or if we are comforted, it is for your comfort, which is effective in the patient enduring of the same sufferings which we also suffer;

1:7

and our hope for you is firmly grounded.

What does comfort mean? _____
_____

2 Thessalonians 2:16-17 says, _____
_____
_____

What does affliction mean? _____

What is the **first** reason for afflictions? _____
_____

We will be able to comfort others because the Father has sent the Holy Spirit *(Paracletos)*, the Comforter, to live within us. John 14:16 says,
_____
_____

What suffering has Paul suffered that is the same as Christ's? _____
_____

1 Peter 4:12-16 says, _____
_____
_____
_____

Note: Look up the word "suffering" in your concordance. First Peter offers a good example of what Paul had in mind.

As our suffering is in abundance so also is our _____
_____

What is the source of comfort? _____

The **second** and **third** reasons for suffering are that the Corinthians
_____
_____

Paul again reminds his family of the principle in 1 Corinthians 12:26f: if one member of the body suffers, the whole body suffers.

Some of the Corinthians had apparently forgotten this principle and were not sensitive to the price that was paid by their pastor so they would be secure in Christ *(see 2 Cor. 11:23-29 for "the tip of the iceberg" so to speak).*

What is the substance of Paul's hope? _____

Firmly grounded has the idea of putting your feet down with your heels dug in.

knowing that as you are sharers of our sufferings, so also you are sharers of our comfort.

1:8

For we do not want you to be unaware, brethren, of our affliction which came to us in Asia,

that we were burdened excessively, beyond our strength, so that we despaired even of life;

1:9

indeed, we had the sentence of death within ourselves so that we would not trust in ourselves, but in God who raises the dead;

1:10

who delivered us from so great a peril of death, and will deliver us, He on whom we have set our hope. And He will yet deliver us,

1:11

you also joining in helping us through your prayers, so that thanks may be given by many persons on our behalf for the favor bestowed on us through the prayers of many.

Knowing is an ongoing knowledge that comes from personal experience.

1 Corinthians 12:26 says, _____
_____
_____

Where was Asia in the first century? _____
_____

When was Paul in Asia? _____

What was this affliction that makes Paul despair of life?
It was: i.   an excessive burden
        ii.   beyond his strength
       iii.   caused despair to the point of death
        iv.   a sentence of death
         v.   included within the sufferings of Christ (v. 5)

But what was it? _____
_____
_____

Here is the **fourth** purpose for suffering - *that* _____
_____

This is the **theme** of the whole book. 2 Corinthians 3:5-6 says, ____
_____
_____
_____
_____

To whom does Paul give the credit for his deliverance? _____
Who is Paul depending on for the future deliverance of perils of death?
_____
Who is HE on whom we have set "our hope"? _____
_____

2 Corinthians 4:7 says, _____
_____

A **fifth** purpose for suffering is that _____
_____
Philippians 4:6 says, _____
_____

A **sixth** purpose for suffering is that _____
_____

1 Thessalonians 5:18 says, _____
_____

PULLING IT ALL BACK TOGETHER - Write a summary of 2 Corinthians 1:3-11:

SPIRITUAL PRINCIPLES

v. 3   We should praise God because He is the source of all mercy shown on us, as well as our comfort.

v. 4   One reason for personal suffering is _____

_____

v. 5   _____

_____

v. 6   Another reason for suffering is _____

_____

v. 7   _____

_____

v. 9   The key to our lives is summarized in the statement: _____

_____

v. 10   _____

_____

v. 11   Two more reasons for personal suffering are _____

_____

SO WHAT? WHAT COULD THIS POSSIBLY MEAN TO ME TODAY?

1.   List the six reasons for suffering mentioned in 2 Corinthians 1:3-11:

_____   _____

_____   _____

_____   _____

2.   What does God promise we can expect from Him during a time of suffering? _____

_____

3.   How do you handle suffering? _____

_____

4.   Suppose you have a friend who was born blind. He seems generally to do very well on a daily basis, but one day become ill and misses several days of work. He begins to get bitter about his inability to move or see, and finally calls out, "What is God doing to me? Why must I suffer one thing after another? It isn't fair!" How would you respond to your friend? _____

_____

_____

THE
NEW COVENANT

DOOMED TO SUCCESS
2 CORINTHIANS 2:12-17

REVIEW

The apostle Paul had traveled to the City of Corinth in or about 50 AD with the hope of bringing the good news of Jesus Christ to a very wicked people. He stayed and taught the scriptures to that people for a year and a half. During that time, he had the joy to express his delight over the fruit of his labor when he wrote this in his first letter to the Corinthians church from Ephesus: "Or do you not know that the unrighteous will not inherit the kingdom of God? Do not be deceived; neither fornicators, nor idolators, nor adulterers, nor effeminate, nor homosexuals, nor thieves, nor the covetous, nor drunkards, nor revilers, nor swindlers will inherit the kingdom of God. Such were some of you; but you were washed, but you were sanctified, but you were justified in the name of the Lord Jesus Christ and in the Spirit of our God" (1 Corinthians 6:9-11).

At the same time, the apostle had received word from the house of Chloe that these new believers were allowing the city's spirit of competition to slip into this new church, as well as the world renowned immorality (1 Corinthians 1:10-17, 5:1-6:20) that permeated the city. Also, soon after Paul had written his first letter (see 2 Corinthians 1:8-11), he was informed that a group of Christian Pharisees called Judaizers hounded the new Gentile believers in Corinth with the false doctrine that "unless you are circumcised according to the custom of Moses you cannot be saved" (Acts 15:1). Their desire was to bring the new Gentile believers under the law of Moses rather than the grace of God.

Those Judaizers also attacked Paul's ministry and undermined his apostleship, so much so that when he sought to return to the city they would not let him teach unless he could produce some letters of reference (2 Corinthians 3:1-3). It was out of this trial that we learn about the difference between false and authentic Christianity. We also learn of the heart of Paul, and the key to his rich life in Christ as experienced through this trial in Turkey: "…we had the sentence of death within ourselves in order that we should no longer trust in ourselves, but in God who raises the dead…" (2 Corinthians 1:8-11).

Second Corinthians 2:12–6:13 provides an outline of the differences between FAKE CHRISTIANITY and AUTHENTIC CHRISTIANITY. At the end of this study, it is our hope that we will know clearly who we are.

CONTEXT

In a very real sense, a serious student of Scripture should read both 1 & 2 Corinthians before starting this section. If you were to read both letters at one sitting you would get a sense that certain sections are out of order and, in reality, there appears to be several letters rather than just two. Keeping in mind that Paul did write several letters to various churches as well as to the church in Corinth, and remembering that most of his letters were written between 50-65 AD, yet were not gathered together into one unit until some time in 90 AD, might help solve some of the confusion.

Maybe this chronological outline will help:

1. Paul starts the Corinthian church in or about 50 AD. (Acts 18:1-17)

2. The apostle leaves after 18 months and goes to Ephesus (Turkey).

3. While in Ephesus he writes a "previous letter" (1 Cor. 5:9, 11) which either no longer exists or may be 2 Corinthians 6:14-7:1 because of the subject of fornicators.

4. Chloe's people arrive with a letter from him to Paul concerning more problems. (1 Cor. 1:11)

5. Paul responds by writing 1 Corinthians and sends it to Corinth via Timothy. (1 Cor. 16:10-11)

6. The problems grow worse. Paul visits Corinth and is rejected by his own people. (2 Cor. 3:1-3)

7. He writes a severe letter. (2 Cor. 10-13)

8. Anxious to hear of the Corinthians' response to his letter he hopes Titus will meet him in Troas. This doesn't occur, so Paul crosses over to northern Greece and meets Titus in Macedonia, and then learns that the Corinthians accepted his loving rebuke. (2 Cor. 7:7-9)

9. He writes 2 Corinthians 1-9 from Philippi—"a letter of reconciliation," without 2 Corinthians 6:14-7:1.*

All chapter headings 16-17-18 and all numbers besides the verses were added centuries later, but are not in the Greek text.

Letter A	Letter B	Letter C	Letter D
Previous letter (mentioned in 5:9, 11 2 Cor. 6:14-7:1 (?)	Corrective letter - 1 Cor.	Severe letter - 2 Cor. 10-13	Reconciliation 2 Cor. 1-9

There are three pressure points of this section (2 Corinthians 2:12–6:13):

1. Paul's position, message and character were challenged by men from Jerusalem. (Acts 15:1-2)

2. The Corinthian church was full of rivalry and sexual immorality. (1 Cor. 1:10-17, 5:1-13)

3. Paul is waiting in Troas for Titus. He is hoping the Corinthians have accepted his severe letter as the disciplining hand of a Loving Father.

The scene is set –

CAMERA...
ACTION...
ROLL'EM!

DOOMED TO SUCCESS

Now when I came to Troas for the gospel of Christ and when a door was opened for me in the Lord, I had no rest for my spirit, not finding Titus my brother; but taking my leave of them, I went on to Macedonia. But thanks be to God, who always leads us in triumph in Christ, and manifests through us the sweet aroma of the knowledge of Him in every place. For we are a fragrance of Christ to God among those who are being saved and among those who are perishing; to the one an aroma from death to death, to the other an aroma from life to life. And who is adequate for these things? For we are not like many, peddling the word of God, but as from sincerity, but as from God, we speak in Christ in the sight of God. (2 Corinthians 2:12-17)

WHAT DOES IT SAY?	*WHAT DID IT MEAN IN THE CORINTHIAN CONTEXT?*
	At this point you want to have before you the following books: 1. A Bible (not a loose translation like *The Living Bible*, *The Message*, or an Amplified edition, but either the NASB or the NIV. 2. A Concordance 3. A book of maps (some Bibles have maps in the back) 4. A Bible dictionary 5. An English dictionary.

2:12 Now when I came to Troas *for* the gospel of Christ	**(I) ALWAYS FULL OF GOOD NEWS** Where was Paul coming from and why? (see Acts 19:40-20:12) ___ _____ _____ _____ _____ The word "for" shows the purpose of the trip. What does "gospel" mean? _____ _____ What is the content of the gospel? By looking up the following verses (we refer to this as a topical study) we can discover the content.

What is the content of the gospel? By looking up the following verses (we refer to this as a topical study) we can discover the content.

Acts 9:19-22	Jesus is the Son of God	v. 20
	Jesus is the Christ	v. 22
Acts 13:16-14:1	Jesus is the Savior	v. 23
	_____	v. ___
	_____	v. ___
	_____	v. ___
	_____	v. ___
Acts 17:16-34	Jesus is resurrected	v. 18
Acts 20:18-35	_____	v. ___
Acts 22:1-21	Jesus the Nazarene is Lord	v. 8
1 Cor. 15:3-4	_____	v. ___
Rom. 1:16-17	*(attitude)* _____	v. ___

and when a door was opened for me in the Lord, not finding Titus my brother,

What door was opened? (see 1 Corinthians 16) To go where? _____
_____
_____

2:13
I had no rest in my spirit...

(I) ALWAYS AT PEACE

I had no rest - The force of this statement could be re-stated: "I had no rest, and I continue to have no rest." In other words, Paul has been, is and remains in this present state of mind.

Paul was hoping he would find Titus so he could find out how the Corinthians reacted to his letter of admonishment.

Who was Titus?: _____
_____
_____

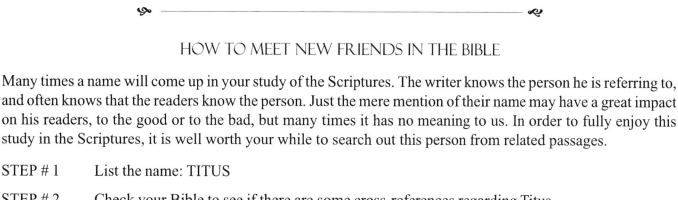

HOW TO MEET NEW FRIENDS IN THE BIBLE

Many times a name will come up in your study of the Scriptures. The writer knows the person he is referring to, and often knows that the readers know the person. Just the mere mention of their name may have a great impact on his readers, to the good or to the bad, but many times it has no meaning to us. In order to fully enjoy this study in the Scriptures, it is well worth your while to search out this person from related passages.

STEP # 1   List the name: TITUS

STEP # 2   Check your Bible to see if there are some cross-references regarding Titus.
For example:

In 2 Corinthians 2:13 there may be a reference to 2 Corinthians 7:6, 13f, which will give you more insight into who Titus is.

Or, simply look up TITUS in your Bible Concordance and it will give you every reference found in the entire Bible.

STEP # 3   TITUS (Ti'-tus) - I found 14 references in the concordance. In order to get a biographical sketch of our mystery person, make a list of the references in chronological order. *WHAT DOES HIS NAME MEAN?*

The references are found in four different epistles (letters), so I need to know the DATES of these epistles in order to establish a true picture of this person. For example, the Peter of Luke 22 (33 AD) is not the same mature person of 1 Peter (65 AD). See a Bible Dictionary for dates.

<u>54 – 56 AD</u>

2 Corinthians 2:13

7:6	_____
7:13	_____
7:14	_____
8:6	_____
8:16	_____
8:23	_____
12:18	_____

<u>55 – 56 AD</u>

Galatians   2:1   _____

2:3   _____

<u>63 – 64 AD</u>

Titus   1:4 _____

<u>64 – 65 AD</u>

2 Timothy   4:10 _____

In the blanks above, fill in the information you have found and also include the meaning of the name TITUS. Many times the meaning of the name gives you insight into their character. Use your Bible dictionary.

STEP # 3   Take all of the above information and see if you can write a letter of reference for Titus *(in other words, see if you can recommend this person for the staff of the* Gentile Crusade for Christ*).*

> *57 AD*
>
> Gentile Crusade for Christ
> PO Box 777
> Corinth, Greece
>
> Dear Sirs:
>
>   I first heard of Titus...

but taking my leave of them,	In spite of the pressure of not finding Titus and not knowing how the Corinthians had reacted to his SEVERE LETTER, he leaves his friends in Troas and goes to Macedonia instead of _____ .

I went on to Macedonia.

Who is *them*? (see Acts 20:4) _____
_____
_____

Where is Macedonia? (Read Acts 20:1-7 for background of this trip)
_____
_____

What happened here the first time he came to town (referred to as his _____ missionary journey)?

List the four major events in Acts 16:9-40:

1. _____
2. _____
3. _____
4. _____

> ⚑   Paul will start to develop for us the characteristic marks of authenthic Christianity vs. the marks of veneer Christianity, or what Paul calls THE OLD COVENANT vs. THE NEW COVENANT.

(3) ALWAYS THANKFUL

Up to this moment the apostle appeared disappointed that his faithful brother Titus had not shown up for their planned meeting in Philippi, Macedonia so they could review the Corinthian's response to his "severe letter." But in 2 Corinthians 2:14, Paul breaks out with a cry of joy: "But thanks be to God." Read 2 Corinthians 7:5-16 in order to discover the source of that joyful heart.

2:14

But

thanks be to God,

Read 1 Thessalonians 5:18 which says: _____
_____

Read Ephesians 5:20 which says: _____
_____

(4) ALWAYS TRIUMPHANT

always leads - Refers to an <u>un</u>conditional fact - he always leads us (not drags us). When we sin, he leads us back into fellowship. He leads us to see where we are wrong, and he works with our free-will and seeks to show us our firm position in him.

who always leads us in triumph in Christ,

"in his triumph" means (see historical note on p. 95) _____

_____

_____

The following is an example of an apparent defeat turned into victory by the hand of God:

> Paul was under house arrest in Rome. This man, who was called to preach the gospel before Kings, Jews and Gentiles, was chained to one of Caesar's prime young men from the elite and politically powerful praetorian guard. Every six hours Paul would experience the changing of the guard, and a new man would be hooked to him. If you want to feel sorry for anyone, feel sorry for the Roman guard. Here he was, living a nice quiet pagan life, and suddenly he pulls guard duty over this most amazing but spiritually disturbing prisoner.

So, because he was locked up by his enemies, God had a chance to do five other things:

1. Phil. 1:12-13: _____
2. Phil 1:14: _____
3. Phil. 1:18: _____
4. Phil 1:19: _____

> Ray Stedman said, "Nero didn't know he was the chairman of the *Advancement of Evangelism* to the Roman empire."

5. Because, when you read Philippians 4:22, it says: _____

_____

_____

What does *sweet aroma* mean? _____

_____

What *knowledge* do you think Paul was referring to? _____

_____

_____

_____

Where is *every place*? _____

_____

_____

and manifests through us the sweet aroma of the knowledge of Him in every place.

2:15
For we are a fragrance of
Christ to God

among those who are being
saved and among those
who are perishing; to the
one an aroma from death to
death, to the other an aroma
from life to life.

2:16
And who is adequate

for these things?

2:17
For we are not like many,
peddling the word of God...

(5) ALWAYS A FRAGRANCE OF CHRIST

Ezekiel 20:41 says, _____
_____

This is always true of our position in Christ. Even when we sin, we are a fragrance to God. Certainly to those around us, the odor of our life changes for the time we are in sin, but Christ is seeking to lead us back into his triumph.

Ephesians 5:2 says, _____
_____

Who are *being saved*? _____

Who is in the process of *perishing*? _____
_____

Authentic Christianity makes people either *better* or *bitter*.

What does *death* mean in Scripture? (See Ephesians 2:1-3) _____
_____
_____

What does *life* mean in Scripture (see John 17:3)? _____
_____

(6) WE KNOW OUR INADEQUACY

What does *adequate* mean? _____
_____

These things refer to:

1 _____

2. _____

3. _____

Paul is going to contrast the ministry of Christ-centered men *vs.* the ministry of self-centered men.

Peddling has the idea of hucksters selling their product on a street corner with the purpose of making money and not caring to get involved with the customer—neither giving a guarantee that the product will do what they claim it will do, nor the promise that they will even be on that same street corner tomorrow. Paul points out that this is their style of life, and that they are doing this with the Word of God. Examples would be:

Acts 8:18-21 (which in essence says) _____

_____

_____

_____

Acts 19:13-16 (which in essence says) _____

_____

_____

_____

HERE PAUL LISTS
FOUR MORE CHARACTERISTICS
THAT CAN BE SEEN IN A GENUINE CHRISTIAN:

but as from sincerity,

(7)   *Sincerity* means _____

_____

but as from God,

(8)   Paul states he is a man with a purpose and a message.

      We speak this way as a style of life. This was and is the only sphere we have any confidence to work in.

we speak

in Christ

(9)   *in Christ*, in the power and authority of the resurrected Lord.

in the sight of God.

(10) *in the sight of God*, with the awareness that every word and action is viewed by the "ever present one."

SUMMARY: IN YOUR OWN WORDS, BRIEFLY SUMMARIZE 2 CORINTHIANS 2:17-17

A BIT OF HISTORY

Because Paul was a Roman citizen, and on a daily basis experienced the presence of the Roman army and its stories of victory, it's possible that in verses 14-16 he had a mental picture of a great spiritual truth.

THE HISTORICAL BACKGROUND

A "triumphal entry" was the highest honor Rome could give to a victorious general. In order to be privileged to participate in this parade, the general had to meet certain conditions:

- He had to be the Supreme Commander on the field of battle.
- The campaign had to be finished, the people pacified, and the troops brought home.
- At least 5,000 of the enemy must have fallen in one battle.
- New territory was gained for the empire.
- The victory had to be over a foreign power, not a civil war.

If these conditions were met, the general was allowed to march in procession through the streets of Rome to the capital, in the following order[1]:

1. The Standard Bearers with the unit's flags.
2. A platform on the shoulders of several men containing the reclining statue of Jupiter, the Supreme God of War.
3. Several platforms on which were placed the spoils of war.
4. Spoils of war (Titus conquered Jerusalem in 70 AD and took the seven-branched candlestick, the golden trumpets, and the golden table of show-bread. These were carried through the streets of Rome during his triumph).
5. Pictures and models of the conquered land and material.
6. The pipers.
7. Several white bulls which would later be sacrificed to the gods.
8. Prisoners of war in chains marching towards death.
9. Horn blowers.
10. Priests swinging the censers with the sweet-smelling incense burning in them.
11. Kings and chieftains placed in carts drawn by oxen.
12. More prisoners.
13. The golden chariot drawn by four white horses, driven by the victorious general. He was dressed in a purple tunic, embroidered with golden palm leaves, and over it a purple toga marked out with golden stars. In his hand he held an ivory scepter with the Roman eagle at the top of it. And over his head a slave held the crown of Jupiter.
14. The general's family.
15. The victorious army fully dressed shouting "lo triumph"!
16. The Roman hierarchy from senators to magistrates.

A once-in-a-lifetime experience!

---

[1]This procession suggested by Wm. Barclay's *Letters to the Corinthians*, p. 204-205, and Moses Hadas, *Imperial Rome*, Time Life Books, p. 58-59.

v. 12   As a Christian I should know the content of the gospel and realize that its truths can change the lives of men and women around me if only I would share those truths. Romans 1:16-17 sets up my attitude.

v. 13   _____
         _____
         _____

v. 14   A main characteristic of a genuine Christian is thankfulness in everything. For example: I'm not thankful for cancer, but thankful that God's hand is behind the cancer and He will bring victory out of apparent defeat.

v. 15   _____
         _____
         _____

v. 16   _____
         _____
         _____

v. 17   _____
         _____
         _____

SO WHAT?   WHAT DOES THIS MEAN TO ME TODAY?

Now, gathering historical information is simple in comparison to applying spiritual truth in life. Scripture was not given to us as a history lesson or mere poetry, but according to 1 Cor. 10:6, 11:

Now these things happened as examples for us, so that we would not crave evil things as they also craved…Now these things happened to them as an example, and they were written for our instruction, upon whom the ends of the ages have come.

Note that Paul took several historical events that happened before his time and says they are for *us*. Scripture is God's revelation of himself and he expects his children to respond. Therefore, the words of God are not to be mastered, *but we are to be mastered by them.*

Now go back over the portion of Scripture you have just studied in 2 Corinthians 2:12-17 and ask yourself the following questions.

1. Is there a command in this section I am asked to obey?

2. Is there a promise from God I can expect to be fulfilled?

3. Is there a sin I am instructed to avoid

4. Is there some danger I can by-pass?

5. Is there a truth I need to ponder?

6. Is there any encouragement I can enjoy?

7. Is there a friend to whom I can pass on what I have learned for his/her encouragement, reproof, correction or instruction?

After you have gathered these truths, ask the Lord to provide the power and wisdom to respond to his great truths, for in them is *life*. Let's try a few of the above principles:

1) What do you think your attitude would be toward a friend who told you he would meet you at the airport at 10 a.m. so you could both fly together to Los Angeles, only now it's 4 p.m. and he never showed up?

_____
_____
_____

2) Now, what was Paul's attitude towards Titus? (Titus 2:11-14) _____

_____
_____
_____

3) Does your attitude and Paul's attitude match? _____

_____

4) If not, why? _____

_____
_____

5) Let's say you have an important meeting at 9 a.m. on Monday morning. You get up on time, get dressed and pray to the Lord that He would use you in this meeting to honor Him. You get in your car and eventually merge onto the highway, checking your watch, and delighted that you will actually arrive 15 minutes early. Then on the radio you hear a traffic report informing you that a tractor trailer has jackknifed and traffic ahead of you will be tied up for at least an hour. You look around hoping for an off ramp only there isn't one and you can't move either way. You finally slow down and know you will be stuck on the highway for at least an hour, and without a cell phone you have no way to contact anyone to tell them you're running late. Basically, you're now at the mercy of the Highway Patrol.

What would have been Paul's reaction to this situation? (See 2 Corinthians 2:14) _____

_____

_____

_____

What would be *your* reaction to this situation? _____

_____

_____

_____

How close was your reaction to biblical truth as expressed in 2 Corinthians 2:14?_____

_____

_____

_____

Now look at the principles expressed in 2 Corinthians 2:15-17 and see how they would help you live out this day. List what you discovered, and *keep it very personal*. _____

_____

_____

_____

_____

_____

_____

_____

_____

_____

_____

_____

_____

_____

_____

_____

_____

_____

_____

_____

_____

ALWAYS TRIUMPHANT!

Some "Tool" Books for a lifetime of Ministry and Discipleship

Authentic Christianity: Living the Life of Faith with Integrity —Ray C. Stedman
© Copyright 1996, Discovery House Publishers, Grand Rapids, MI; ISBN 1572930179

Case for Christ, The —Lee Strobel
© Copyright 1998, Zondervan, Grand Rapids, MI; ISBN 0310209307

Case for Faith, The —Lee Strobel
© Copyright 2000, Zondervan, Grand Rapids, MI; ISBN 0310234697

Celebration of Discipline: The Path to Spiritual Growth —Richard J. Foster
© Copyright 1988, HarperSanFrancisco, San Francisco, CA; ISBN 0060628391

Cost of Discipleship, The —Dietrich Bonhoeffer
1st Touchstone Edition, © Copyright 1995, Touchstone: Simon & Schuster, New York, NY; ISBN 0684815001

Daily Study Bible Series, The —William Barclay
Westminster John Knox Press, Louisville, KY. (Multiple volumes.)

Devotional Classics —Richard J. Foster and J. B. Smith
© Copyright 1993, HarperSanFrancisco, San Francisco, CA; ISBN 0060669667

Foundations of the Christian Faith —James Montgomery Boice
2nd Edition, © Copyright 1986, InterVarsity Press, Downers Grove, IL; ISBN 0877849919

Master Plan of Evangelism, The —Robert E. Coleman
2nd Abridged Edition © Copyright 1994, Revell Books: Baker Publishing Group, Grand Rapids, MI; ISBN 0800786246

New Joy of Teaching Discovery Bible Study, The —Oletta Wald
New Revised Edition © Copyright 2002, Augsburg Fortress Publishers, Minneapolis, MN; ISBN 80664429X

New Strong's Exhaustive Concordance of the Bible, The —James Strong
© Copyright 1991, Nelson Reference: Thomas Nelson, Inc., Nashville, TN; ISBN 078526096X

New Unger's Bible Dictionary, The —Merrill F. Unger, R.K. Harrison (Editor)
© Copyright 1988, Moody Publishers, Chicago, IL; ISBN 0802490379

NIV Harmony of the Gospels —Robert L. Thomas and Stanley N. Gundry (Editor)
© Copyright 1988, HarperSanFrancisco, San Francisco, CA; ISBN 0060635231

So, You Want To Be Like Christ? Eight Essentials to Get You There —Charles R. Swindoll
© Copyright 2005, W Publishing Group: Thomas Nelson, Inc., Nashville, TN; ISBN 084991731X

Vine's Complete Expository Dictionary of Old and New Testament Words —W.E. Vine, Merrill F. Unger
© Copyright 1996, Nelson Reference: A Division of Thomas Nelson, Inc., Nashville, TN; ISBN 0785211608

Made in the USA
Charleston, SC
30 September 2011